CRITICAL APPROACHES TO THE PSYCHOLOGY OF EMOTION

This fascinating book explores the different methodologies, resources and strategies that have been used to study emotion, and identifies emerging trends and research perspectives in the field.

Emotion is a subject that has been thoroughly investigated in all fields of social and behavioural sciences. And yet the more we have attempted to individualize emotions and set limits that separate the different types of emotions, the more the subject has resisted these categorizations. Mapping the changes and diverse perspectives in the study of emotion, author Simone Belli explores how a critical psychology of emotion has emerged in order to answer this paradox, examining emotions within a social framework. Divided into five chapters, the book uses interdisciplinary critical approaches to cover everything from the interaction between emotion and language, to emotional contagion such as the spread of fear in a pandemic. There is also a particular focus on emotion analysis in digital environments, which have left a deep mark on our lives from the beginning of this century.

Showcasing a selection of important investigations that have dealt with the study of emotions in society, *Critical Approaches to the Psychology of Emotion* is essential reading for students of critical social psychology, sociolinguistics, sociology, anthropology and philosophy.

Simone Belli is Professor of Social Psychology at the Complutense University of Madrid. His research is focused on understanding why emotions have a strong relationship with language, and how it is possible to express these emotions in online/offline spaces and intercultural contexts.

CONCEPTS FOR CRITICAL PSYCHOLOGY: DISCIPLINARY BOUNDARIES RE-THOUGHT

Series editor: Ian Parker

Developments inside psychology that question the history of the discipline and the way it functions in society have led many psychologists to look outside the discipline for new ideas. This series draws on cutting edge critiques from just outside psychology in order to complement and question critical arguments emerging inside. The authors provide new perspectives on subjectivity from disciplinary debates and cultural phenomena adjacent to traditional studies of the individual.

The books in the series are useful for advanced level undergraduate and postgraduate students, researchers and lecturers in psychology and other related disciplines such as cultural studies, geography, literary theory, philosophy, psychotherapy, social work and sociology.

Most recently published titles:

Developing Minds
Psychology, neoliberalism and power
Elise Klein

Marxism and Psychoanalysis
In or against Psychology?
David Pavón-Cuéllar

For more information about this series, please visit: www.routledge.com/Concepts-for-Critical-Psychology/book-series/CONCEPTSCRIT

CRITICAL APPROACHES TO THE PSYCHOLOGY OF EMOTION

Simone Belli

LONDON AND NEW YORK

Designed cover image: Getty

First published 2023
by Routledge
4 Park Square, Milton Park, Abingdon, Oxon OX14 4RN

and by Routledge
605 Third Avenue, New York, NY 10158

Routledge is an imprint of the Taylor & Francis Group, an informa business

© 2023 Simone Belli

The right of Simone Belli to be identified as author of this work has been asserted in accordance with sections 77 and 78 of the Copyright, Designs and Patents Act 1988.

All rights reserved. No part of this book may be reprinted or reproduced or utilised in any form or by any electronic, mechanical, or other means, now known or hereafter invented, including photocopying and recording, or in any information storage or retrieval system, without permission in writing from the publishers.

Trademark notice: Product or corporate names may be trademarks or registered trademarks, and are used only for identification and explanation without intent to infringe.

British Library Cataloguing-in-Publication Data
A catalogue record for this book is available from the British Library

ISBN: 978-1-032-16311-6 (hbk)
ISBN: 978-1-032-16309-3 (pbk)
ISBN: 978-1-003-24799-9 (ebk)

DOI: 10.4324/9781003247999

Typeset in Bembo
by Newgen Publishing UK

CONTENTS

Preface   *vii*

Introduction   1

1   Emotions and language: The discursive turn   4
   1.1   More spontaneous than artificial, more sincere than thoughtful 5
   1.2   The philosophical and psychological character of the emotion 6
   1.3   The construction of the emotion 7
   1.4   Narratives of our emotions 8
   1.5   Toward a performative perspective 11
   1.6   Emotions over time 13
   1.7   Conclusion 15

2   Emotional affordance: The socio-material turn   19
   2.1   About the affordance: an introduction 20
   2.2   The emotional affordance 21
   2.3   Technology and emotional affordance 22
   2.4   Emotional affordance in social networks 23
   2.5   Be happy and positive 25
   2.6   Conclusion 26

3   The gamification of emotions: The digital turn   31
   3.1   The psychology of happiness 32
   3.2   A new context for sharing emotions 33
   3.3   The gamification of our emotions 34

    3.4   Emotions in social networks 37
    3.5   Towards a hybrid theory? 41
    3.6   Conclusion 44

4   Between the collectivity of emotions and emotional contagion: The social turn   52
    4.1   Collectivities and movements 52
    4.2   Recognition, imitation, and performance 56
    4.3   The emotional contagion 58
    4.4   Fear and trust, or a new mode of existence of the subject 59
    4.5   Conclusion 61

5   Working with emotions: The management turn   66
    5.1   Career and collaboration in research 67
    5.2   Emotional leadership in science 71
    5.3   Conclusion 74

Conclusion   77

Index   79

PREFACE

Psychologists are too often tempted to make the same intuitive commonsensical mistake about the nature of 'emotion' as the ordinary folk they learn from and then try to educate with a more sophisticated and empirically-grounded version of the same story about ourselves – that emotions are deep down inside our human nature and deep down inside each individual, inside the individual subject of psychological research whose responses are gathered together and accumulated, tabulated and then distributed according to what the psychologist thinks they know about personality types.

Critical psychologists know better, but their suspicion that something is wrong with the individualist assumptions that underpin and govern the discipline often fall short of persuading us that there is a better account to be had of what emotions are. There is a body of scientific analysis and theoretical work at the edges of psychology about 'emotion' that enables us to build a better account, a good deal of it inspired or illuminated by the work of the 'realist' philosopher of science Rom Harré. Simone Belli has learned from and worked with Harré, and now brings a careful considered critique of the mainstream models to bear on a number of different domains in which 'emotion' is a guiding – and often limiting – thread. And, more than that, this book gathers together and synthesizes a fully social approach to emotion that will be invaluable to critical psychologists wanting to dig into the conceptual roots of the discipline.

We feel emotion and it is crucial to remember that we also 'perform' it. Emotion is for others as much as it is for each of our individual selves, and here we have the conceptual basis for a fully social constructionist approach to emotion that is also embodied, grounded in what we know about social relationships from outside psychology and what we also know about embodiment and biology from disciplines adjacent to but usually misunderstood by mainstream psychologists.

Emotion is felt to be deep inside us even when we are performing emotion in a network of 'affordances' that are profoundly collective, and that then has consequences for when we are online or when we are at work, when we navigate the affordances of digital environments or when we are managed by others. We feel emotion to be deep inside as part of the illusion of possessive individualism that lies at the basis of modern psychology, an individualism that tells us that what we think and feel are ours, as if they are possessions, as if our very individuality is under threat if it is to be acknowledged as moulded by collective processes, by society.

This book, *Critical Approaches to the Psychology of Emotion*, gives us a performative critical approach to emotion that is grounded in good scientific inquiry and in a host of empirical studies, and it succeeds because it is always sceptical, doubting, at a distance from the usual mistaken assumptions that govern the discipline. It is inside psychology and working outside it, 'outwith' it. This is very much in keeping with the reality of emotion itself, something that is somewhere at the border between the interior space of our bodies and what is required of us in the social networks that make us human.

Ian Parker
University of Manchester

INTRODUCTION

This book refers to the different methodologies, resources, and strategies that have been used to study emotions in the last decades. The aim of this book is to identify new trends and research perspectives in research on emotion from a critical perspective. The book would provide readers with a range of different investigations that have dealt with the study of emotions in different contexts. It also especially focuses on emotion analysis in digital environments, which have left a deep mark on our lives from the beginning of this century.

This mapping would take into account certain elements in order to not leave the epistemic space that it is intended to study the emotions. Moreover, it presents the changes and diverse perspectives that still exist today when studying an emotion and how critical psychology of emotions emerged in order to understand them in the social framework. It was evident that in all fields of social and behavioural sciences, the subject of emotions has been investigated, raised, criticized, and experimented with. The book delimits this subject by following few but important hypotheses through the work that researchers have done in these years.

The book is divided into five chapters or turns. The unifying thread through it is the critical paradox that the more one tries to individualize emotions and set limits that separate the different types of emotions (e.g. affects, passions, moods, feelings and states of mind), the more evident that it is an unnecessary systematization. These distinctions just deal with different ways of feeling. We continue with the same perspective when it comes to establishing boundaries between different affective states, where scientists are still far away from reaching full consensus between these different ways of feeling. Our interest in the study of emotions shares the integration of different disciplines of psychology and social science in what is called social constructionism. Many authors have contributed with their studies to the consolidation of the basis that our emotions are discursively and socially constructed.

This can only be fully understood in reference to the social and cultural contexts in which they occur.

In the first chapter, we will introduce the complexity of the study of emotions in social sciences from the discursive turn. We explore aspects that unify the perspective of different authors about the relationship between emotions and language linking our emotions to our stories, narratives that evoke our emotions. Thanks to these narratives, emotions emerge and can be easily recognized also by subjects who are not experiencing them. The process of speaking about oneself and accessing emotions requires theoretical frameworks that divide thinking from feeling, and different emotions are also reified, turned into things (Parker, 2007). Emotions are thus internalized through social and discursive practices, but the critical link that connects both elements is language. Our statement in this chapter is that to communicate emotions means putting 'something' in common between human beings. Emotions are that 'something'.

In the second chapter, the main focus will be on affordance, a key concept in recent years for the study of emotions in socio-material interaction. Many current theories take emotions to be fundamentally embodied (e.g., Prinz, 2004; Maiese, 2011; Hutto, 2012; Colombetti, 2014). Embodied accounts aim to understand emotions as evolved complex patterns of bodily reactions whose biological function is to respond to situations of urgent concern. The bodily reactions involved in emotions partly constitute the emotions' being meaningful, because emotions are the result of an adaptive history in which the bodily responses became reliable responses to urgent situations (Hufendiek, 2017). Equally, with the arrival of the socio-material turn in our daily and professional practices, emotions have also followed this transformation process, or at least the way we refer to them through language. When we share our emotions using technologies, we connect online with the analogue space where our bodies are, since what happens and is expressed in the online world is also felt in the offline world. The process of testing emotions in different spaces makes, in the end, the analogue body the only recipient of these emotions, since all these different emotions will always be experimented through it. The socio-material turn of emotions introduces a concept that in the last decade has allowed us to understand how these environments design the multiple emotions that a subject can experience in these spaces, that is, the concept of affordance.

In the third chapter, we present the digital turn that has affected different areas of our lives, also modifying the way we interact and constituting new types of social relationship. Our interest is in the study of emotions in digital contexts, especially in the affective sphere and its variants. We claim that the contemporary society in which we live is based on social norms that privilege sharing well-being, happiness, and our positive emotions and experiences. Social media is just a reflection of our society, and they ask us to follow exactly these same emotional patterns, as we will observe with different examples.

In the fourth chapter, we introduce the social turn to observe how the emotions in collectives are structurally complex and are socially distributed. In this chapter, we examine the collectivity and the sharing of emotions in society, a concept that has worried psychologists and social scientists in recent years. We present here different perspectives and settings where these emotions can be studied, from social movements to artistic companies. We present our research of collectivity of emotions and emotional contagion in different groups that have been analyzed, and the communicative and synchronization dynamics that underlie subjective processes. A greater understanding of the emotions of the members of a team would greatly limit errors and accidents when thinking about the creative and professional process of the entire activity. We conclude this chapter with the example from the pandemic time that we are currently living. A diffuse, dispersed, and liquid shared emotion, in this case the fear, is perfect to understand the emotional contagion in society.

In the last chapter, we conclude our analysis of emotions by observing how these work in professional contexts like academia, introducing the management turn of emotions. With a critical perspective, we analyse emotions that academics and researchers feel every day in their institutional spaces like laboratories and offices, and how they manage these. We explore the emotional dimension of the strategies that researchers use to collaborate and cooperate between themselves. Hence, we highlight that the emotional work of researchers consists in combining different emotional strategies by activating and deactivating affection, warmth, and spontaneity, in their professional interactions.

We consider five turns to map a territory of how it is possible to do research in the psychology of emotions not following a mainstream perspective. These turns help us to connect with a critical point of view the fruits of this conjuncture and the many different examples of approaches that study emotions in different contexts. As Ibáñez and Iñiguez (1997) say, what gives the new wave of critical psychology is that critical psychologists have developed methods and knowledge-producing paradigms of their own that can challenge the mainstream on its own terms both empirically and productively. These developments in critical psychology are cause enough for celebration as it becomes clear that these new turns have started to challenge the mainstream traditions.

References

Colombetti, G. (2014). *The Feeling Body. Affective Science Meets the Enactive Mind*. Cambridge, MA: MIT Press.
Hufendiek, R. (2017). Affordances and the normativity of emotions. *Synthese*, 194(11), 4455–4476.
Hutto, D. (2012). Truly enactive emotion. *Emotion Review*, 4(2), 176–181.
Ibáñez, T., & Iñiguez., L. (1997). *Critical Social Psychology*. London: Sage.
Maiese, M. (2011). *Embodiment, Emotion and Cognition*. Basingstoke: Palgrave Macmillan.
Parker, I. (2007). *Revolution in Psychology: Alienation to Emancipation*. London: Pluto Press.
Prinz, J. (2004). *Gut Reactions. A Perceptual Theory of Emotion*. Oxford: Oxford University Press.

1
EMOTIONS AND LANGUAGE
The discursive turn

In this first chapter, we will introduce the complexity of the study of emotions, exploring aspects that unify the perspective of different authors about the relationship between emotions and language introducing the so-called discursive turn. This turn allows us to understand how our emotions are linked to our stories, narratives that evoke our emotions. Thanks to these, emotions emerge and can be easily recognized also by subjects who are not experiencing them directly. The process of speaking about oneself and accessing emotions requires a theoretical framework that divides thinking from feeling, and different emotions are also reified, turned into things (Parker, 2007). Emotions are thus internalized through social and discursive practices, but the critical link that connects both elements is language. The discursive turn of emotions is one of the main important turns in a critical psychology of emotions, and is rooted in a productive research paradigm and not just a form of critique (Ibañez & Iñiguez, 1997). Our statement in this chapter is that to communicate emotions means putting 'something' in common between human beings. Emotions are that 'something'.

We start this book highlighting the eternal paradox that the more one tries to separate the emotions from them and set limits that separate the different types of emotions of the affections, passions, feelings, and moods, the more evident that this is an unnecessary systematization (Guedes & Álvaro, 2010). These distinctions are equivalent, all dealing with different ways of feeling. We try to not standardize the array of 'emotions' that comprise the reduced table of senses that psychology textbooks sample and theorize about, usually confined to sections devoted to 'emotion and motivation' (Lara, 2020). We continue with the same perspective when establishing the boundaries between the various affective states, where scientists are still a long way from reaching full consensus between these different ways of feeling (Evans, 2003). Our interest in the study of emotions shares the integration of different disciplines of the social sciences in what is called social constructionism

DOI: 10.4324/9781003247999-2

and that many authors have contributed with their studies to the consolidation of the basis that our emotions are constructed discursively and socially, and that can be fully understood only in reference to the social and cultural context in which they occur (Gergen, 1985; Harré, 1986a; Harré & Parrott, 1996; Ovejero, 2000).

1.1 More spontaneous than artificial, more sincere than thoughtful

The figure of Rom Harré has always been one of the most prominent references in the field of the study of emotions from the discursive turn. In the last two interviews with the New Zealand scientist before his death in 2019, Harré continued to insist that emotions are strictly linked to the words that define them (Dierolf, 2013; Belli, Aceros & Harré, 2015). In his last academic phase at Georgetown University, Harré worked on ways to accommodate disciplines in the study of emotions, such as neuroscience with psychology, without reducing the latter to the former (Christensen, 2019). In this way the study of emotions would not be a very different branch of psychology as an aspect of life where meanings and biology interact with our moral sense about what is right or wrong. For example, anger and the act of getting angry is the demonstration of reasoning about something bad that has happened to us and about what we have the right, and even the duty, to protest.

The concern about the rise of biological reductionism that some neuroscientists have maintained throughout the last decades to the present is evident; the sociocultural structure in the generation of emotions is very important (Crespo, 2018). This is an alarm that becomes evident when in a science that is explicitly defined as 'social' there is practically no reflection on the sociability of individuals and their political condition, leaving completely isolated the emotions from the subjects. With the same critical perspective, we raise the radical dependence on emotions in the constitution of all subjectivity (Fernández Villanueva, 2018). A critical social psychology of emotions must take into account that people are relational, intersubjective microstructures, built with and from the social. And consequently, it cannot focus solely on positivist disciplines such as neuroscience or basic psychology. In this first chapter, we analyze the dominant definitions of emotions that focus mainly on the physiological and expressive correlations of some basic emotions that need to introduce complex emotions, feelings, emotional states, and even moral feelings. All of this is nuanced by the interpretation of situations and contexts and the production of narratives of these experiences.

These different perspectives have in common the close and evident relationship between emotions and language, since emotions can only be expressed through it, both verbally and non-verbally (Belli, Harré & Iñiguez, 2014). One of the most influential scientist of emotions, Arlie Hochschild (2016), shows how our emotions are linked to our stories, that is, narratives that evoke our emotions. Also from the philosophy, Peter Goldie (2012) emphasizes how, thanks to these narratives, emotions emerge and can be easily recognized also by subjects who are not experiencing them. In addition, the regulation of emotions, a topic that has captured the attention of many psychologists in recent years, has been characterized by understanding emotions as epistemic spaces (Belli & Broncano, 2017). Emotions are thus internalized through social and discursive practices. The basic association that links both elements, communication (both verbal and non-verbal) and emotions, is based on language.

For over one hundred years, emotions have been studied in several disciplines in the humanities and social sciences, and there exists a large number of different theoretical approaches. It is usually considered that emotions are natural body-experiences that are then expressed through language, and that language, in turn, is often described as irrational and subjective. That is, what we first feel in our bodies, later comes out of our mouths in the form of a discourse which is, in some way, opposed to reason. Psychology tries to ward off anything in human experience that could not be observed and measured, dividing between reason and feeling (Parker, 2007). Emotions are also said to be gestated in the unconscious and not in the will. Thus, they are more spontaneous than artificial, more 'sincere' than 'thoughtful'.

In psychology, Mayor (1988) argues that there is no commonly accepted definition of emotion, and the history of emotions must be seen in the context of changes in psychology as a discipline. In fact, one could say that what has most influenced the study of emotions has been the continuous change experienced by psychology throughout its development as a discipline. And these will also influence the other two areas of the study of emotions: philosophy and sociology. Research of emotions that does not take account of these disciplines, will give just a superficial view. Subsequently, the focus has been on the language-emotion tandem. Efforts have been made to develop arguments that serve to differentiate the relationship between these two terms; i.e. if the emotions can be 'located' in language or they can be accessed through language (Harré & Finlay-Jones, 1986).

Given the multiplicity of perspectives, and the open and plural theoretical and methodological controversies, as already mentioned, we will offer an overview of the scientific study of emotions as a continuous line of different contributions.

1.2 The philosophical and psychological character of the emotion

William Lyons (1985) provides a good starting point to introduce the discursive turn from the philosophy of emotion. Lyons defines emotion as a functional model expressed in words. Thus, emotions are feelings directed outward and toward what causes them to come out. In this case, Lyons assumes the concept of emotions as formulated by Spinoza, who asserted that we often have false beliefs about the causes of our feelings, which lead us to hate those we should love and vice versa.

The emotion of love illustrates this quite clearly. According to Lyons (1985), we use words as indicators of the presence or absence of love. We say things like 'don't you love me anymore?' when the other person has not shown certain feelings in settings where he or she was expected to do so. Similarly, when someone tells us 'I don't feel the same for you', we can infer that it means 'I don't love you anymore'. It is not easy to declare our love for someone, especially if one hopes to be taken seriously and, at the same time, one tries to keep distance from the evaluative aspects of love held by the beloved.

According to Wittgenstein (1958), we produce spontaneous linguistic articulations of our feelings and impressions of the world. We express descriptive states of our affects. Wittgenstein asserts that phrases are made up processes, away from the consecration of words and emotions. In the same vein, there are new methods of the post-empirical psychology paradigm that has been discussed in Harré's (1989) work. There is a blurred line between philosophy and psychology, especially when it comes to frame an area of knowledge such as emotions and language. For this reason, we do not want to set as a goal a demarcation between the two disciplines. We opt for a continuous interplay between them, which allows us to see an interesting set of contributions.

Likewise, many authors working in this area prefer a mainstream approach. Some of them approach the behaviourist tradition, which focuses on interactions via observation. They follow the methodological standards of quantitative and positivist approaches. These authors assert that the best way to establish causal relationships is to consider that behaviour is actualized in a social context. Mandler (1975) argues that psychology of emotions should address the conditions that give rise to cognitive and physiological events. It should offer an integrative perspective of the cognitivist and behaviourist approaches as parts of one psychology of emotions. It should gather contributions that have been studied separately.

The psychology of emotions is a discipline that has given ample space to the study of emotion in the last two centuries. It is important to understand these different perspectives in the scientific context in which they have been produced. Nevertheless, each of them has contributed to and influenced considerably the topic of emotion viewed as a social and discursive construction in different ways. Thanks to the aforementioned scientific field, we find it more comprehensible to understand how the study of emotion has had a distinct and complementary 'history' in over a hundred years. This allows us to provide some common coordinates for the understanding of the following sections.

1.3 The construction of the emotion

Keith Oatley (2007) argues that in the history of writing, emotions have been the source of most interesting arguments. Above all, there is an emotion that is the most commonly used in the history of writing; this emotion is love. Let us think for a moment of an emotional expression: 'I love you'. This sentence is used to express love for another person, the most famous examples being those of romantic novels. In these novels, authors try to introduce emotions in words; some authors succeed, others do not. Nevertheless, this process might be seen inversely. Some authors attempt to construct emotions through the use of words. They construct a context, and give meaning to certain words, so we can talk about love. As we shall see later, they try to construct love as an emotional performance.

The great writers are continually fighting to put emotions into their pages. They do their best to represent the different aspects of love. It is impossible to relive a great love, or to interpret the non-verbal signs of love. When a person says, 'I love you', there is no turning back, it is a sign of no return between two people. When one of these people pronounces these three words, the situation between them irremediably changes, positively or negatively. We try to relive the great passion of love, but paradoxically it seems that we cannot. Nevertheless, the use of certain words and the construction of certain contexts, allow us to recreate this performance. We can narrate this great passion, though we cannot relive it. Although it is not possible to relive it, it is possible to reconstruct this particular mood by using words. We can construct purely emotional situations, only through the use of language.

When it comes to this 'wordy' love issue, another fascinating topic is the interpretation of the great romances, i.e. the interpretation of signs, looks, gestures, which are very tenuous in performance. But, as we saw in previous paragraphs, those signs are part of the body language and express emotions. Gestures, signs, and glances are weak, as they exist at the very moment of their own expression and then they disappear. And if they attempt to repeat themselves in order to achieve the same effect they are doomed to fail. Repetition is useless, it means nothing but a repetition of the phrase 'I love you'. Saying 'I love you' is understood as an emotional performance, even if well done, i.e. saying it while caressing the neck and the ear of the beloved one. The expression of an emotion is not just a statement, but a complete performance. 'I love you' is an expression of the whole body, not just a simple sentence.

The way and form of performance, like being shy for instance, has several effects on the actual performance itself. An 'I love you' said by a shy person is not the same 'I love you' said by a self-confident person. The words are the same, but the two performances are really distinct from each other, since persons do not express their emotion by just uttering it, but by uttering it in a certain way (Green, 1970). Words are designed to produce real emotions, which might exist in the intersubjective space and in the subjective interpretation of these signs.

Since emotions are socially produced, they have a close relationship with language and communication (Searle, 1992). It has to do with the discovery of the social character of mind, which links semantics and linguistic pragmatics to our field of action, as discursive social psychology states. The social construction of emotion allows us to speak of emotions as something that can be communicated.

1.4 Narratives of our emotions

Narratives construct emotions that weave through societal history and bring to the fore certain aspects of society in our lives. Narratives are the instruments for understanding these emotions, as we have said before. They have two different roles: one is to describe a situation, the other is to justify what we learn and make happen in our lives. Hutto (2008) claims that folk psychology narratives make sense of intentional actions in our lives. Human beings learn about own emotions thanks to own narratives from when we are children to the present. Emotion is not a scientific or technical concept; everybody knows what emotions are without studying them like a psychologist does.

Following Harré (2009), the grammatical subject of most words used to describe emotion is the person, because the person is angry, sad, proud, chagrined, joyful, and so on. There is no such thing as embarrassment, but there are plenty of embarrassed people. So people's narratives are composed of an emotion grammar to describe emotions. In emotion grammar, people make use of such concepts as 'love', 'jealously', 'trust', and so on. This type of grammar changes in every context and includes semantic and syntactic rules and storylines. Thanks to the work of philosophers and psychologists, we now have concepts to explain these emotion processes or constructions – these narratives. The narratives allow to us to understand how such phrases as 'being angry', 'being jealous', and 'being ashamed' are compared. Ryle (1949) argued that a mood like 'sadness' is a complex of dispositions to feel, do, and say certain sorts of things. All these things are metaprocesses, which at the same time include meta-emotions as we will see later. Each component is indispensable to being (and to feeling) sad. Language is a tool of emotional life that helps to modify and solidify emotional activity (Mendonça, 2008). It is also a creative tool for handling emotional difficulties in our lives.

Another essential point for understanding why narratives are important for our emotions are the temporal patterns. According to Goldie (2012), people don't feel the same emotion over time, because time changes, the context changes, and we observe emotions through an external perspective on what happened. Goldie introduces the internal/external standpoint, which we can observe in this narrative:

> Last week, that person said things very important and intimate to me; I trust him, and he trusts me enough to confide in me. Today, when I remember that event, I discover that I love him, and not just trust him.

In my external standpoint narrative (today about an event that happened last week), we discover an internal emotion, love. We find a sort of emotional gap, or a retrospective emotion that we did not have at the time (last week), or that was probably caused by this situation of trust. It is an action of rethinking the past in order to change the present. In emotional narratives we go through this action many times: something happens in the past, and it has a different meaning when we re-elaborate it in the present. So, emotions are singular experiential episodes at discrete points in time, in response to specific events (Rogers, Schröder, & von Scheve, 2014). For Mendonça (2008), these episodes provide tools for continually questioning and exploring the emotional world, our constellation of emotions.

We agree with Goldie that narratives are causal accounts; for example: 'When you grieve, you often look back on the past, on your time with the person you loved, knowing now what you did not know then: that the person you loved is now dead' (2012, 65). Causal accounts are not mechanical processes where A causes B, and B causes C. Causal accounts in narratives are like A causes B or C, and B probably produces C or returns to A. In this sense, causal accounts in narratives show our constellation of emotions. Love is the basis of this new emotion of grief, while in previous examples trust is the basis of the new emotion of love. It is always an emotion about an emotional process. In an essay on gay liberation, Britt & Heise (2000) trace the emergence of pride from shame via affect-control processes involving fear and anger. This social movement revolves around efforts to transform shame into pride.

Losing a loved person entails sorrow, sadness, hopelessness and disrupted social functioning (Bonanno & Kaltman, 2001). Over time, the bereaved is usually able to pass certain milestones such as learning to manage painful emotions, recreate or strengthen relationships and restore a sense of purpose (Goveas & Shear, 2020). The literature has outlined how the traumatic circumstances of a loved one's death may negatively impact the bereavement process (Cipolletta, Entilli, Bettio, & De Leo, 2021; Kristensen et al., 2012; Neimeyer & Burke, 2017): reactions to traumatic deaths usually involve rumination, avoidance, an intense yearning to be with the loved one and, most of all, difficulty to accept the loss (Howarth, 2011).

Grief is an inescapable human experience (Walter, 2000) as well as a social emotion, which emerges from relationships and attachments (Jakoby, 2012). The bereaved are required to perform an emotional role in line with socially and culturally charged scripts (Jakoby, 2012). This resonates with Hochschild's (1983) concept of emotion work: the sustained efforts individuals make to cultivate emotional responses that fit the feeling rules of roles or situations, and then demonstrate these in ways that honour localized display rules. Emotion work may be performed either positively, by showing false sentiments that one does not sincerely feel, or negatively, by denying or suppressing feelings that are subjectively true (Scott, 2019).

For Velleman (2001), emotion is something temporal that unfolds differently over time. But it is a performance with certain temporal patterns involving circumstances, physiological reactions, and biological changes: a form of structured episodes. For Harris (1989), these episodes mark an important step in emotional development. These narratives work in a causal account, where they don't appear just as a single event but instead appear as one thing happening after another, where everything is interconnected. Love, trust, and grief are interconnected, and it is impossible to mention one without mentioning one or both of the others. They circulate, and it doesn't matter which emotion appears first, because it is not possible to separate them. Looking on the past, constructing a narrative, there are actions that allow us to recognize these emotions and meta-emotions and to put them into words. These combinations and interactions of emotions are crucial to action (Jasper, 2011). For Wollheim (1999), interactions are embedded in the narratives that we associate our emotions with, where we have to learn to identify our emotions early in life. A narrative then has these two aims: to describe our world and to justify and make sense of our experience.

Thanks to a narrative account we can analyze the complexity of emotions. In love or jealousy narratives we can find the 'facts' (McIsaac & Eich, 2004). These facts contain experiences of loss of trust or having trust. These facts are 'structured episodes' in our narratives, and they are composed of elements of emotional experience: thought, feeling, bodily change, expression, and so forth (Goldie, 2012). In the narratives of Freud's patients, anxiety appears as a meta-emotion of the first-order emotion of fear of death in their dramatic episodes. In autobiographical episodes, we use a rather journalistic style to report what happens to us. Meta-emotions allow us to structure these episodes and to argue which emotions we have experienced in a particular circumstance.

Goldie (2012) insists that narrative expression should not necessarily be seen as a discursive device but rather be seen as a combination of that which is spoken, written, drawn, acted, sung, mimed, danced, filmed, and otherwise communicated through. These narratives make human lives intelligible (Broncano, 2008). Narratives are the ultimate structures of our lives (Zahavi, 2005), because we live out narratives in our lives and understand our own lives in terms of such narratives (Broncano, 2008). For Mendonça (2008), these narratives incorporate a dynamic nature and are never finished.

We argue that experiences before narratives are crucial for understanding the emotional relevance of stories. It is for this reason that emotions are open-ended. They are open because emotions change the impact they have 'as time goes by' and are subject to multiple modes of revision (Mendonça, 2008). We are biologically programmed to experience affects and feelings but are culturally shaped to experience emotions. We live in a historical time because our identity is culturally shaped as a narrative (Broncano, 2008), and these narratives give sense to our life, in a continuing agency.

1.5 Toward a performative perspective

We have shown how constructionism helps us to understand how emotions are constructed through language. Now we will focus on the psychological aspects of such a process. Psychology has contributed, in recent decades, to situate emotions in a new space called 'discursive psychology of emotion' (Edwards, 1997, 1999). In discursive psychology of emotion the most important issue is the use of emotions in language, specifically the actions and effects of emotional speech in relational frameworks (Buttny, 1993).

In order to understand discursive psychology, it is necessary to return to some authors with a social constructionist background as, for instance, the contributions of Harré (1986a). Despite their agreement, discursive psychology and social constructionism have some differences. While discursive psychology has focused on the role of discourse, social constructionism has put its emphasis on social relations and their context (Cortina, 2004). Lakoff (1980) and Wierzbicka (2008) have made significant contributions to discursive psychology, proposing a cognitive-semantic model. Gergen (1994) finds a significant relationship between these two major perspectives and proposes the cognitive-semantic and social constructionist model.

According to Edwards (1999) the psychology of emotions is the study of how they are used and are important emotional terms in everyday speech. This definition is widely argued (Edwards, 1997, 2000) and shared (Harré, 1999). Edwards (2000, 2001) explores how emotional discourses produce strong reactions in interactions that are perceived as emotional reactions. But emotions can't be studied as purely empirical in the discourses in which they are been generated (Lara, 2020). When Wetherell claims 'with affective practice rather than circulating emotion as the unit of analysis, relationality would re-appear' (2015: 160), she is only talking about a relationality that is empirically accessible for her. For Ali Lara (2020), practice is affective and emotional. Not only because practice is the pure manifestation of a process of affecting and being affected, but also, the communicative capacities of the body and the transmission of affect are actualized through practices as nonconscious components of the affective process.

Judith Butler (1993, 1997) deals with emotions and affects as a constant evolution in practice. She looks at emotions in a completely new perspective through the concept of performance. Although in her text the term 'emotion' is not explicit, it arises spontaneously in all of her discourses and positions. Using the concept of performance, she explores how discourse creates a need for affects and emotions. In this way, emotions are a performance produced by constructions, which are internally discontinuous acts. That is to say, emotions do not exist prior to their performance, and success of the copy, or 'repetition' of an emotion previously performed, can never be invoked to faithfully reproduce that event, i.e. a new emotion. These events or constructions are seen as natural by repeating over time a set of multiple everyday life interactions. These performative acts are open to constant change and redefinitions. Acts (Butler, 1993) eventually become standards that can be seen as natural.

The notion of performance in Butler's work is indebted to John Austin (1955). When she mentions the concept of performativity in language, certainly we must mention John Austin's work, especially one of his most famous works *How to Do Things with Words* (1955). Austin distinguished three types of acts that can be done with words, called locutionary, illocutionary, and perlocutionary. Saying something is a locutionary act, but at the same time it is an illocutionary act and sometimes a perlocutionary one. Butler is interested in perlocutionary acts that establish that saying is doing. Saying something generates effects and consequences on feelings, on thoughts and actions, on self, and on others. Austin referred to feelings and emotions contained in conventional performative acts, and illocutionary aspects produced in a performative way. The notion of performance used by Judith Butler, continues to be a locutionary act. The implicit point in Austin's work is that performance depends on 'happy' utterances, i.e. when its structure is part of its circumstances. Butler takes this notion and widens it, giving it the strength and power that these actions have on the speaker and on others and, above all, their capacity to produce intended changes and transformations.

The concept of performativity in Butler is therefore an attempt to find a way to rethink the relationship between social structures and individual agencies. In Butler's interpretation, performativity is understood as that which promotes and supports the implementation process through an iterative repetition subject to certain rules. The politics of performativity requires the iterative power of discourse to produce the phenomenon of emotion, since emotion does not exist before one says something, i.e. before producing a speech act. Thus, emotions are designed as socially constructed phenomena. They are socially constructed identities that indicate how the audience must behave (Butler, 1993). As explained above, these emotions do not pre-exist their performance, and cannot be reused and categorized and quoted in the future (Gregson & Rose, 2000: 438).

Performative acts are constructed by iteration, by persistence and stability, and by the possibility of rupture, of change, of deconstruction too. However, performance is not just an actuation, a staging. According to Butler, iteration introduces at once the temporality of a subject. It is not a singular act or event, but a ritualized production, an iteration of a ban under certain conditions, a taboo, Butler argues that what constitutes the real strength of performance is not consistent with the formulation of any of them. However, both views, taken together, led to the proposal of a theory of social iterative speech acts. Speech is not like writing, says Butler, because the body is present in speech in a different way than in writing, but also because the relationship between body and speech, though oblique, actualizes in the same expression. Although writing and speaking are both acts of the body, the mark of the body that reads a text does not always make clear who owns the body. The speech act actualizes in the body. The simultaneity of the production and externalization of expression not only report what is said but shows the body as the instrument for the expression of the emotions. Then, the relation between speech act and body act puts into its rightful place the body, its gestures, its aesthetic, and its emotions. So acts, gestures, and codes in general are performative in the sense that the essences and identities expressed are fabrications manufactured and sustained through corporeal signs and other discursive means (Butler, 1993). It does not mean that for Butler the body is reducible to language but that language and, consequently, emotions emerge from the body. Finally, in order to externalize an emotion a sentence is not enough, a complete performance is needed. 'I love you' is an expression of the body as a totality, not just a simple phrase.

1.6 Emotions over time

In this last part of the chapter, and after having defined the various steps for understanding the relationship between emotions and language, especially following the concept of performance, we will now focus on the meaning of all this, and what are the 'effects' in everyday discourse. In discursive psychology and in social constructionism there are two perspectives, the historical and the discursive. In the historical, emotions change over time, and such a change is due to discourse. Performance helps us to understand why some emotions appear and others disappear in ordinary language, since emotions are narratives, they are action stories of our time (Oatley & Jenkins, 1992: 75).

For Harré (Belli, Aceros, Harré, 2015), the main framework for introducing the social and historical context into psychological research is in the work of Lev

Vygotsky. We can never complete a psychological research programme because the phenomena we are trying to map and the language with which we are doing this is continually changing. The dog cannot catch its tail but is always hopeful of doing so. Over the centuries we will generate a sequence of 'psychologies' that will need interpretation because the ways of thinking and the language and other symbolic means will be ever changing. We take this for granted in studies of religion – Latin is not the language of modern Christian thought, but unless we understand it, we will not be able to understand the great authors of the Middle Ages. Recent studies of Shakespeare's plays sensitive to the vastly different world view and taken-for-granted beliefs, have led to very different readings of those psychologically profound works.

Emotions are a bodily experience that cannot be separated from the sociocultural contexts in which we find ourselves; of course experience is never the same in different bodies. This is why we consider it important to see how emotions change over the years. It is a way to understand emotions in a historical-discursive framework, and to see the changes into time. This vision can also be understood as a performance in everyday discourse. There are emotional terms which our generation no longer uses, but other terms are used which have replaced earlier ones in the discursive arena. Thus, emotions become obsolete, outdated, completely 'out'. Emotions evolve or disappear over time and are always led by the concept of performance in our daily stories. Each language offers us examples of emotions that have disappeared, that are not in our discourse anymore. For example, the term 'accidie' is extinct in the discursive arena.

In use from the thirteenth century until the sixteenth century, today the term accidie is synonym of laziness, disinterest, but is not equivalent to any of them. Accidie refers to feelings associated with loss of intrinsic motivation towards our own religious duties (Robert, 2003: 245). In literature one can find the term 'accidie' in 'Don Quixote', by Cervantes. The term accidie has been rescued in recent years by Giorgio Agamben (1995) to describe the state that lies between mourning and melancholy:

> Throughout the Middle Ages, a scourge worse than the plague that infects castles, the villas, and palaces of the city's world tilts on the houses of the spiritual life, enters the cells and in the cloisters of monasteries in the tebaidas of hermits in the rags of the prisoners. *Acedia, tristitia, taedium vitae, desidia* are the names that the Fathers of the Church gives to induce death in the soul.

Accidie also belongs to the seven deadly sins, and it was often related to God (Edwards, 1997). But in our days it is completely missing as an emotion, and it is very difficult to find it in everyday discourse (Harré, 1986b).

Another example is the term 'melancholy'. Our ancestors made frequent use of this word many times to express a certain emotion, but our generations do not (Robert, 2003: 160). It is very easy to remember our grandparents pronouncing this term in their stories, but we no longer use it. It seems that melancholy has gone out of fashion, disappearing in our everyday discourse. Neither does it appear in songs, even though in a not too distant past this term was frequently used. Melancholy is now replaced in everyday language with words such as sadness, depression, and loneliness.

These two examples were used to support the theory that emotions have to be interpreted in the social context in which they occur. Thus, it is no wonder that emotions come and go in the discursive arena. It is a steady performance that makes new feelings appear in the discursive arena.

1.7 Conclusion

As we already said, emotions have a strong relationship with language. We can express emotions through language. Thus, we believe it is essential to show how different disciplines have made important contributions to this theory. It is important to understand that it is impossible to speak of the social construction of emotions without taking into account this background and these contributions. We understand emotions in this chapter as a textual practice, as a semantic evolution. Thus, some of the aims of a researcher in this field would be to find in emotional discourse forms of contemporary life. We understand that performance is subject to the power of the discourse of emotions. Emotional discourse contains new concepts and metaphors to articulate and understand emotions in the lexicon.

Robert (2003: 160) argues that emotions create actions, especially those concerning the words that generate them. In this sense, emotions, or words referring to emotions, are not the same in a classroom at the University of Chicago or in a monastery in the medieval Spain (Roberts, 2003: 183). They change over time and space, i.e. they change depending on the context in which they are generated. Emotions change in natural and spontaneous language of everyday life. New words enter the discursive arena, thanks to a performance that has never been tried before, and then new areas are produced. For instance, emotions begin to enter the technological language as another performance in everyday discourse. Love stories in front of a flat screen are typical of everyday life as we will observe in chapter three. Since emotions are bodily experiences that cannot be separated from the sociocultural contexts in which we find ourselves, we consider it important to emphasize that emotions have changed over the years. Emotions have to be understood in a historical perspective in order to see their changes in time. Why do emotions become obsolete, outdated, completely out? Emotions evolve or disappear over time, and so does performance in our daily stories. Each language offers us examples of emotions that have disappeared, that no longer exist in our discourse.

As we have said throughout this chapter, expressing emotions means putting something in common with others. We have also seen how an emotional performance, such as love, changes through historical discourse. Regarding performance, love always depends on the non-verbal gestures, and how the other responds. Something in these gestures, in its performance, does not get repeated in the same way. Such gestures cannot pass the word. Everything becomes real in the intersubjective emotional space. Thanks to the concept of performance, developed by Judith Butler, emotions are not something fixed, defined, and static. They are constantly evolving, continuously complying with an iteration process, and they do it through language, natural and subjective. This constant iteration makes emotions appear and disappear from the discursive arena, leaving some forgotten and discovering new others. We consider emotions as a constant evolution in daily discourse.

References

Agamben, G. (1995). *Homo sacer: il potere sovrano e la nuda vita*. Bologna: Einaudi.
Austin, J. (1955 (1998)). *How To Do Things with Words*. Cambridge: Cambridge University Press.
Belli, S., Aceros, J., & Harré, R. (2015). 'It's all discursive!' Crossing boundaries and crossing words with Rom Harré. *Universitas Psychologica*, 14(2), 771–784. https://doi.org/10.11144/Javeriana.upsy14-2.iadc
Belli, S. & Broncano, F. (2017). Trust as a meta-emotion. *Metaphilosophy*, 48(4), 430–448. https://doi.org/10.1111/meta.12255
Belli, S., Harré, R., & Iñiguez, L. (2014). Narratives from call shop users: Emotional performance of velocity. *Human Affairs*, 24(2), 215–231. https://doi.org/10.2478/s13374-014-0221-1
Bonanno, G.A., & Kaltman, S. (2001). The varieties of grief experience. *Clinical Psychology Review*, 21, 705–734. https://doi.org/10.1016/s0272-7358(00)00062-3
Britt, L. & Heise, D. (2000). From shame to pride in identity politics. *Self, Identity, and Social Movements*, 5, 252–268.
Broncano, F. (2008). Trusting others. *Theoria*, 61, 11–22.
Butler, J. (1993). *Bodies That Matter: On the Discursive Limits of Sex*. London: Routledge.
Butler, J. (1997). *Excitable Speech: A Politics of The Performative*. London: Routledge.
Buttny, R. (1993). *Social Accountability in Communication*. London: Sage Publications.
Christensen, B.A. (ed.). (2019). *The Second Cognitive Revolution: A Tribute to Rom Harré*. London: Springer Nature. https://doi.org/10.1007/978-3-030-26680-6
Cipolletta, S., Entilli, L., Bettio, F., & De Leo, D. (2021). Live-chat support for people bereaved by suicide. *Crisis*, 3(2), 98–104.
Cortina, A. (2004). The jealousy passion: A semiotic discourse analysis. *Alfa: Revista de Linguistica*, 48(2), 79–94.
Crespo Suárez, E. (2018). Un enfoque social sobre las emociones. In J. Álvaro (ed.), *La Interacción Social: Escritos En Homenaje A José Ramón Torregrosa* (pp. 165–183). Madrid: Centro de Investigaciones Sociológicas (CIS).
Dierolf, K. (2013). The new psychology: discursive practices, not internal forces – an interview with Rom Harré. *InterAction*, 4(2), 78–85.
Edwards, D. (1997). *Discourse and Cognition*. London: Sage Publications.
Edwards, D. (1999). Emotion discourse. *Culture & Psychology*, 5(3), 271–291. https://doi.org/10.1177/ 1354067X9953001
Edwards, D. (2000). Extreme case formulations: Softeners, investment, and doing nonliteral. *Research on Language & Social Interaction*, 33(4), 347–373.
Evans, D. (2003). *Emotion. A Very Short Introduction*. Oxford, Oxford University Press. https://doi.org/10.1093/actrade/9780192804617.001.0001
Fernández Villanueva, C. (2018). De la interacción social a la subjetividad. In J. Álvaro (ed.), *La Interacción Social: Escritos En Homenaje A José Ramón Torregrosa* (pp. 217–233). Madrid: Centro de Investigaciones Sociológicas (CIS).

Gergen, K.J. (1985). The social constructionist movement in modern psychology. *American Psychologist*, 40, 266–275. https://doi.org/10.1037/0003-066X.40.3.266
Gergen, K. (1994). *Realities and Relationship*. Cambridge: Harvard University Press.
Goldie, P. (2012). *The Mess Inside: Narrative, Emotion, and the Mind*. New York: Oxford University Press.
Goveas, J.S., & Shear, M.K. (2020). Grief and the COVID-19 pandemic in older adults. *The American Journal of Geriatric Psychiatry*, 28, 1119–1125. https://doi.org/10.1016/j.jagp.2020.06.021
Green, O. (1970). The expression of emotion. *Mind*, 5, 551–568.
Gregson, N., & Rose, G. (2000). Taking Butler elsewhere: Performativities, spatialities and subjectivities. *Environment and Planning D*, 18(4), 433–452.
Guedes Gondim, S.M. & Álvaro Estramiana, J.L. (2010). Naturaleza y cultura en el estudio de las emociones. *Revista Española De Sociología*, 13, 31–47.
Harré, R. (1986a). *The Social Construction of Emotions*, Oxford: Basil Blackwell.
Harré, R. (1986b). *Varieties of Realism: A Rationale for the Natural Sciences*. London: Blackwell.
Harré, R. (1989). Language and the science of psychology. *Journal of Social Behavior & Personality*, 4(3), 165–188.
Harré, R. (1999). The rediscovery of the human mind: The discursive approach. *Asian Journal of Social Psychology*, 2(1), 43–62.
Harré, R. (2009). Saving critical realism. *Journal for the Theory of Social Behaviour*, 39(2), 129–143.
Harré, R., & Finlay-Jones, R. (1986). Emotion talk across times. In Harré, R. (ed.) *The Social Construction of Emotions* (pp. 220–223). London: Sage Publications Inc.
Harré, R., & Parrott, W.G. (1996). *The Emotions. Social, Cultural and Biological Dimensions*. London: Sage Publications.
Harris, P.L. (1989). *Children and Emotion: The Development of Psychological Understanding*. Oxford: Basil Blackwell.
Hochschild, A.R. (1983). *The Managed Heart: Commercialization of Human Feeling*. Berkeley, CA: University of California Press.
Hochschild, A.R. (2016). *Strangers in Their Own Land: Anger and Mourning on the American Right*. New York: The New Press.
Howarth, R. (2011). Concepts and controversies in grief and loss. *Journal of Mental Health Counseling*, 33, 4–10. https://doi.org/10.17744/mehc.33.1.900m56162888u737
Hutto, D. (2008). *Folk Psychological Narratives: The Sociocultural Basis of Understanding Reasons*. Cambridge, MA: MIT Press.
Ibáñez, T. Iñiguez., L. (1997). *Critical Social Psychology*. London: Sage.
Jakoby, N. (2012). Grief as a social emotion: Theoretical perspectives. *Death Studies* 36(8): 679–711.
Jasper, J. (2011). Emotions and social movements: Twenty years of theory and research. *Annual Review of Sociology*, 37, 285–303.
Kristensen, P., Weisæth, L., & Heir, T. (2012). Bereavement and mental health after sudden and violent losses: A review. *Psychiatry: Interpersonal and Biological Processes*, 75, 76–97. https://doi.org/10.1521/psyc.2012.75.1.76
Lakoff, G. (1980). *Metaphors We Live By*. Chicago: University of Chicago Press.
Lara, A. (2020). *Decentering Subjectivity in Everyday Eating and Drinking: Digesting Reality*. London: Routledge.
Lyons, W. (1985). *Emotion*. Cambridge: Cambridge University Press.
Mandler, G. (1975). *Mind and Emotion*. New York: Wiley.
Mayor, L. (1988). *Psicología De La Emoción. Teoría Básica E Investigaciones*. Valencia: Promolibro.

McIsaac, H., & Eich, E. (2004). Vantage point in traumatic memory. *Psychological Science*, 15(4), 248–253.
Mendonça, D. (2008). Let's talk about emotions. *Thinking: The Journal of Philosophy for Children*, 19 , 2–3.
Neimeyer, R.A., & Burke, L.A. (2017). Spiritual distress and depression in bereavement: A meaning-oriented contribution. *Journal of Rational-Emotive & Cognitive-Behavior Therapy*, 35, 38–59. https://doi.org/10.1007/s10942-017-0262-6
Oatley, K. (2007). *Breve Storia Delle Emozioni*. Bologna: Il Mulino.
Oatley, K., & Jenkins, J.M. (1992). Human emotions: Function and dysfunction. *Annual Review of Psychology*, 43, 55–85.
Ovejero, A. (2000). Emotions: Reflections from a socioconstructionist perspective. *Psicothema*, 12, 16–24.
Parker, I. (2007). *Revolution In Psychology: Alienation to Emancipation*. London: Pluto Press.
Roberts, R.C. (2003). *Emotions: An Essay in Aid of Moral Psychology*. Cambridge: Cambridge University Press.
Rogers, K., Schröder T., & von Scheve, C. (2014). Dissecting the sociality of emotion: A multilevel approach. *Emotion Review*, 6(2), 1–10.
Ryle, G. (1949). *The Concept of Mind*. New York: Barnes and Noble.
Scott, S. (2019) *The Social Life of Nothing: Silence, Invisibility and Emptiness in Tales of Lost Experience*. London: Routledge.
Searle, J.R. (1992). *The Rediscovery of The Mind*. Cambridge: MIT press.
Velleman, D. (2001). The genesis of shame. *Philosophy and Public Affairs*, 30(1), 27–52.
Walter, T. (2000). Grief narratives: The role of medicine in the policing of grief. *Anthropology & Medicine*, 7(1), 97–114.
Wetherell, M. (2015). Trends in the turn to affect: A social psychological critique. *Body & Society*, 21(2): 139–166.
Wierzbicka, A. (2008). A conceptual basis for research into emotions and bilingualism. *Bilingualism: Language and Cognition*, 11(02), 193–195.
Wittgenstein, L. (1958). *Philosophical Investigations*. Oxford: Basil Blackwell.
Wollheim, R. 1999. *On the Emotions*. New Haven: Yale University Press.
Zahavi, D. (2005). *Subjectivity and Selfhood: Investigating the First-Person Perspective*. Cambridge, MA: MIT Press.

2
EMOTIONAL AFFORDANCE
The socio-material turn

Thanks to the concept of performance, we have introduced in the previous chapter the emotions as a constant evolution in our speeches showing different examples in everyday interactions. In this second chapter, the main focus will be on affordance. We have observed how current studies take emotions to be embodied (Prinz, 2007; Maiese, 2011; Hutto, 2008; Colombetti, 2014) and the corporal responses involved in emotions partially constitute the emotions being meaningful. Emotions are the product of an adaptive history in which the corporal reactions became reliable responses to critical situations (Hufendiek, 2017). With the arrival of the so-called digital transformation in our daily and professional practices, emotions have also followed this transformation process, embodying the body with the technological devices. When we share our emotions via digital technologies, we connect digitally with the analogue space where our bodies are, since what happens and is expressed in the online world is also felt in the offline world. The process of sharing emotions in different spaces makes, in the end, the analogue body the only recipient of these emotions, since all these different emotions will always be experimented through it. The socio-material turn of emotions introduces a concept that in the last decade has allowed us to understand how these digital environments design the multiple emotions that a subject can experience in these spaces, that is, the concept of affordance.

In this chapter, the idea of affordance as a feeling and being 'in the world' appears in the field of the study of emotions from a critical perspective in psychology. We focus on digital environments that can evoke certain emotions in them. The study of affordance has tended to overlook these emotional elements of the relationship between subjects and objects. The qualities of objects, including digital technologies, are associated with specific emotional experiences of their users in what we call the socio-material turn of the emotions. We present the affordance of emotions in social interactions to understand the ways in which people recognize and conceive society and the artefacts present in it. We propose the term emotional affordance to better include the emotional characteristics of technological objects, keeping an eye on the virtues of technological environments to move towards more nuanced theories at the connection of social activities and technological materiality.

2.1 About the affordance: an introduction

Research in the relationship of psychology and technology in the last decade is focusing the consequence of emotions, communication, and corporality, but the concept of the affordance may be one way to combine and connect these different elements. A socio-material turn tries to appreciate the fundamental entanglement of the material and the social in humans' actions. This offers understandings on the significance of emotional processes in socio-material network composed by subjects and objects.

Hufendiek (2017) suggests that affordances can be defined as standing in multi-faceted interactions to each other, and that these interactions can account for what has been considered as the emotions being subject to rational norms. Norman's (1999) introduction of affordances goes some way to answering how an item can afford a subject through a chance to choose it and to interact with it. Affordance has offered between social construction and technological determinism, an adjustment that made it possible to point to the corporality or purposes of technology by identification that these tasks are permanently involved in the actions of actors (Graves, 2007; Neff, Jordan, McVeigh-Schultz, & Gillespie, 2012; Nagy & Neff, 2015).

Parchoma (2014) introduce the notion of 'technological affordance', studying the connections between society and its technologies. Studying political and social consequences of technological innovations, researchers have assumed growth to a technological determinist perspective that holds that technologies 'actively cause new forms of social relations to come about' (Hutchby, 2001: 442). Subject–object debates highlight challenging speeches on interactions among objects and social practices. Gibson considers of affordances as items that are of value to the understanding organism:

> The perceiving of an affordance is not a process of perceiving a value-free physical object to which meaning is somehow added in a way that no one has been able to agree upon; it is a process of perceiving a value-rich ecological object. Physics may be value-free, but ecology is not.
>
> *Gibson, 1986:140*

Emotions can be assumed as representations of affordances that are not only deliberate but also intentional, including a specific manner of expertly answering to and thereby grasping social properties. However, emotions might be intentional without thereby involving complex representations with abstract content; rather, they may be planned merely because the skilful corporal responses that organize one for action constitute a certain manner of demonstration (Hufendiek, 2017).

Affordances are partly established by properties of the situation, since they can originate to be perceived by the organism; yet affordances fundamentally contain a response-dependent component (Hufendiek, 2017).

2.2 The emotional affordance

The socio-material turn of emotions allows us to understand how the affordance perceived in these digital environments can be extended to the emotional sphere. One of the first psychologists that adopted this perspective was Derek Edwards (1999), using the concept of 'rhetorical affordance' to show in what way emotion is used discursively. Emotions can be treated also as unintentional responses, as internal states, or social demonstrations. We focus which affords certain options for our engagement (Brown and Stenner, 2009). Such an affordance for engagement implies a precognitive plane of collaboration in which the body is already responding; it has concluded its own activity, and it is already acting upon the items, affecting and being affected (Lara, 2020). For example in conflicts, emotions play a key function in determining social responses to conflicting events (Bodtker & Katz Jameson, 2001).

We present the Hufendiek's example (2017: 4465) to introduce this emotional affordance:

> A new predator might enter the environment of a species and would constitute a danger even if no member of the species has the ability to represent this danger. The dodo is an example of a bird that was endemic to the island of Mauritius where it evolved in isolation from predators and as a result happened to be not only flightless but also fearless. The bird became extinct briefly after sailors introduced rats and other animals on the island in the seventeenth century that plundered dodo nests. Dodos had no naturally evolved abilities to detect these predators and defend themselves or fly. Nevertheless it makes sense to say that the predators were dangerous for the dodos.

For Hufendiek (2017), 'being dangerous' is a relational property that can be instantiated autonomously of a species' being able to response to that property has the benefit that it can account for the adaptive difficulty that the property might place on the species.

These situations only exist sometime in the record of a species, it is difficult to conceive a creature in a situation where risk is never instantiated. 'Being in danger' looks to be a property that deserves the label of a 'core relational theme' (Hufendiek, 2017). Being alive implies the probability of being in danger.

Emotions include an extensive variety of sentiments from negative to positive, both with exclusive features and discursive affordances (Edwards, 1999; Potter & Hepburn, 2007). Meredith and Stokoe (2014) observe that participants in digital contexts adapt to analogous inclinations to those in social interaction. They show the affordances of the digital technology and how these are positioned by users.

While the technology permits for the editing of messages, the ways in which users do this has certainly not been observed in a naturally occurring context. They have presented that while users do edit messages prior to sending, they do not take time to check spelling before sending these. This has clear implications for understanding how a technological affordance can affect an interaction (Meredith & Stokoe, 2014). Users in digital settings do not create new modes of communication, merely recreate and adapt types of communication from the analogic context (Benwell & Stokoe, 2006).

2.3 Technology and emotional affordance

Technologies can provide predictable emotional stimuli in relation to the congruence between their calculated characteristics and the users expectations (Wood and Moreau, 2006; Chaudhuri et al., 2010; Sage et al. 2019). This concept of the emotional strength of technologies as reducible to their calculated features, stems from a neglect of both social approaches to emotions and technology. For Bruno Latour (1999, 2004), it is more important in his Actor-Network Theory (ANT) how these different aspects connect between other actors instead of differentiating them. That is, 'how one is affected' (Latour, 1999: 22) through 'objects, properties, fears, techniques that make us do things unto others' (Latour, 1999: 25). Latour (1999) defines 'good' physical connections among actors that 'make existence possible' (p. 29) while 'bad' connections are those that 'kill' actors (p. 30). Action is understandable throughout patterns of good and bad connections rather than in analyses of confined connection versus independent detachment (Latour, 1999). Latour's (1999, 2004) idea of connection guarantees to adopt questions of emotions frequently unamenable to ANT exploration, containing: how are actors affected to join and be joined in assistance of a technology, or how and why do actors study to become perceptive to new actors, and their emotional longings, as well as their precise interests? Latour's answer is that 'To understand the activity of subjects, their emotions, their passions, we must turn our attention to that which attaches and activates them' (Latour, 1999: 27).

In a research on emotional affordance using digital technology in professional settings (Belli, 2021), it was observed how a specific tool used to elaborate texts in a collaborative way, like Google Docs and Dropbox, can offer new affordances to researchers to facilitate collaboration, affording in-built qualities for communication and sharing. The affordance of these two diverse technologies is pretty comparable – sharing and working connected with files – but the emotional connection is diverse. The first one, Google Docs, permits many scholars to work at the same time on an online document, which causes different difficulties for users. This file can produce no positive emotional connection among users, the document, and the rest of the socio-material network. On the other hand, in Dropbox, users edit a file that can be left in the depository, and users have the chronology of the file. Researchers are sure to not miss significant information. The emotional connection in the socio-material network can predict the practice that technology offers to the users. Tools' qualities can prevent or encourage collaborations with other users. This socio-material network creates the emotional connection where we can distinguish negative and positive emotions. Darics and Gatti (2019) observe how technological issues are discussed with participants sharing practices and giving information to each other. These interactional events were chances to share support and empathy (Crider & Ganesh, 2004).

The interaction between human and technology is largely determined by the emotions experienced by its connected users. The design of these digital environments can induce certain emotions in them (Mick & Fournier, 1998; Thüring & Mahlke, 2007; Lim et al., 2008). The study of affordance has tended to observe these emotional features of the relationship between technologies and users. Emotional situations influence how individuals recognize the setting and perform activities. For example, anxiety reduces the precision of data processing and worsens the correctness of the awareness of affordance ability (Bootsma, Bakker, van Snippenberg & Tdlohreg, 1992). While emotional circumstances have been studied in technology design research, they are infrequently combined into the way we think about affordance. The virtues of tools, including digital ones, are associated with certain emotional practices of their users. Characteristics of technological objects can perform as emotional evidences. Users may understanding that technologies have emotions or are socio-material actors and connect with these objects as if the objects were social actors (Reeves & Nass, 1996; Nass & Moon, 2000). They can form emotional associations with tools and can project certain emotions, considering them as social beings (Turkle, 2004). The psychology of emotions has a leading role in this new context, helping to build tools and digital environments that are better adapted to the expectations and emotional perceptions of users (Saariluoma & Jokinen, 2014).

2.4 Emotional affordance in social networks

Thanks to emotional affordance, approaches to materiality within intersubjective processes emerge that require richer and more nuanced notions to study the spaces mediated by digital technologies. Once established, either by nature or by design of the technological environment, emotional affordance becomes the way subjects feel and act in digital interactions. In social psychology, affordance is the result of the interaction between tools and users, and depends both on the perception of the tool by users and on their qualities or characteristics. It would be about identifying the ability of human beings to figure their communicative settings and, therefore, do what they perceive. For example, in the social network Facebook there are a defined number of possibilities for interaction between users. This digital platform offers to its members the possibility to make some decisions to impact their networks, which profiles their emotions of the mediated setting. The creators of this environment have incorporated different emotions in their tool, deciding what possible emotions their users will be able to feel and share. For any post in Facebook, users can decide what to feel by pushing a button: Happiness, Love, Surprise, Anger, and Sadness.

As Mark Zuckerberg, the creator of Facebook, stated in an interview published in 2014 in *Newsweek*:

> The like button is really valuable because it's a way for you to very quickly express a positive emotion or sentiment when someone puts themselves out there and shares something. Some people have asked for a Dislike button because they want to be able to say, 'That thing isn't good'. That's not something that we think is good. We're not going to build that, and I don't think there needs to be a voting mechanism on Facebook about whether posts are good or bad. I don't think that's socially very valuable or good for the community to help people share the important moments in their lives.

We can understand, thanks to this extract, how creators of digital platforms can design and shape the emotions that users can experiment with in these digital environments. The emotional affordance can be different for each platform we use, irrespective of the intended purpose of its creators. With respect to most emotions, there is no evidence to make certain claims about the source of these emotions.

Waterloo et al.'s (2018) study analyzes the dominant injunctive types of emotion expression on four social media platforms (Twitter, Instagram, Facebook, and WhatsApp). The study analyzes the communication of negative and positive emotions and points to link their perceived relevance on the diverse social platforms. For Waterloo et al. (2017), social media platforms support emotional self-expression, inviting users to frequently update their emotions and experiences on their networks. Affordances are part of a multifaceted context and as such are connected to each other, and gives us a justification of why certain emotional reactions (such as envy) only make sense in reaction to others and why some emotional reactions (such as envying oneself) never make sense but are strictly illogical (Hufendiek, 2017).

Research has exposed that the communication of positive emotions is perceived as more suitable than negative emotion expression (Caltabiano & Smithson, 1983). The motive for this is that negative emotions are apparently more intimate and therefore seen as disturbed performance when pointed at strangers (Chaikin & Derlega, 1974; Howell & Conway, 1990). Three qualities can be used to describe a platform, which involve social privacy settings, its following-mechanism, and mood. Social privacy is described as the extent to which a behaviour is achieved in a private or public setting (Lapinski & Rimal, 2005). Associated to this is the subsequent mechanism that a platform affords: mutual or nonmutual. Mutual following occurs when two users need to accept each other in their network, while nonmutual succeeding allows a user to follow another without that user having to follow in return (Davenport et al., 2014; Lup et al., 2015). The principal modalities of content that a platform offers describe the type of content that is shared. The mixture of these three features helps differentiate how normative shapes of emotion expression potentially differ among Twitter, Instagram, Facebook, and WhatsApp.

There are specific studies that show how a digital platform affords emotions. For example, Utz and Beukeboom (2011) demonstrate how Facebook can have a destructive effect on romantic relationships, encouraging romantic jealousy. After relationships end, Facebook can allow unhealthy surveillance of the ex-partner and delay emotional recovery (Marshall, 2012; Fox, Jones et al., 2013; Fox & Warber, 2014). While social reaction can be accepted privately, most of it is recognizable to other users. If the social response is positive, such as receiving 'likes' after posting a photo of a new dress, it is likely the participant will have a positive response or experience self-affirmation (Toma & Hancock, 2013). Because Facebook affords constant availability and updating, users often cited a 'fear of missing out' on a new post that they felt was important (Przybylski, Murayama, DeHaan, & Gladwell, 2013). These comments indicate that Facebook makes relationship maintenance suitable, its perceived accessibility and the visibility of these interactions may raise expectations. If partners' Facebook use or expectations are not compatible, this creates disagreement, and relationship maintenance on the site feels troublesome (Fox & Moreland, 2015). Digital spaces offer an important emotional resource for users, both in their design and in relationship to the users. These spaces afford certain behaviours that can aid in managing mood by being designed for actions that are favourable, away from causes of anxiety, and enjoyable to the users.

Newett et al. (2017) show how the digital app to find partners, Tinder, is used as a digital meeting place. This digital space was deemed to offer a wider range of hypothetical partners than offline spaces. Tinder's digital space is not only connected but is also analogous to the user's physical settings insofar as where a person who they digitally may meet is physically, to an extent.

2.5 Be happy and positive

Numerous studies have analyzed cultural and social changes that involve psychology discourses, such as 'positive thinking' and the role of 'positive' emotions in influencing social relations (Illouz, 2008; Ahmed, 2010; Hochschild, 2012; Sotgiu, 2013). This view analyzes the tricky assumptions of recent methods of quantifying for happiness as an object (Cromby, 2011). In these studies, happiness can be understood as a device that localizes psychological experiences as individual affairs, governed by a cognitive processes (Martínez-Guzmán & Lara, 2019).

Greco and Stenner (2013) argue that the notion of happiness splits the individual from the world, studying how happiness discourses and practices in the framework of positive psychology can shape distinct subjectivities and foster specific relationships individuals have with themselves. This perspective studies the psychology of happiness (Sotgiu, 2013) in the context of social, cultural, and political changes in late capitalism. Binkley's work has located the psychology of happiness over methods of individualism shaped by the neoliberal context. This change contains an erosion of the passive individual dependent on external and institutional psychological authorities in favour of an autonomous individual with an entrepreneurial spirit, ready for self-government (Serrano-Pascual & Carretero-García, 2022). It contains the passage of a model positioned on psychological regulation to a rationality consisting of a self-regulated subject devoted in the maximization of his psychological and emotional capital (Martínez-Guzmán & Lara, 2019). These studies seems to be marked by approaches to the research of subjectivity as it emerges out of material relations (Clough, 2018; Lara et al., 2017) and the political implications of what the multiple technologies of control societies do to human bodies (Clough & Willse, 2011; Massumi, 2015; Protevi, 2009).

The idea of happiness means the production of a body that feels frequently anxious, at some points stressed, because it should be enthusiastically working for its happiness. The psychology of happiness is neither an evaluation of the past nor the final product of a work dynamic. Ahmed (2010) explains that psychology of happiness is a promise, and it is mandatory that it is never fulfilled.

Binkley (2014) suggests that adjusting the temporalization of the individual is the source throughout which psychology of happiness brings the individual to the logic of a neoliberal economy. Happiness, and the temporalization of government, is an intensification of power's production of subjectivity (Martínez-Guzmán & Lara, 2019). This pre-emptive temporality is exactly what psychology's regime of happiness does, as Ahmed explains: 'positive psychology involves the instrumentalization of happiness as a technique. Happiness becomes a means to an end, as well as the end of the means' (2010: 10). The happiness regime is consistent with practices of subjectification of neoliberal governmentality, as it operates as an individualized, and self-applied device, targeting a subject tied to a rationality of continuous self-evaluation and systematic enhancement. It shows how these technologies are internalized in the body and how they reach affective processes beyond the realm of the unified subject and conscious behaviours and desires (Martínez-Guzmán & Lara, 2019).

2.6 Conclusion

For Hufendiek (2017), emotions are about affordances such as a danger-to-be-avoided. Emotions' aboutness is organized by the physical reactions they involve. These physical reactions are set up by development and a learning history to respond to social properties such as 'being dangerous'. Assuming that emotions are about objectively existing relational properties, permits for the claim that these properties can be instantiated and individuated regardless of whether the organism is able to perceive them (Hufendiek, 2017).

Emotions are not only about something, but they also present their objects in a particular manner. The manner in which an emotional object is given to us is what is named the intentionality of emotions. The shape of bodily responses that fosters in response to a relational property turns this property into an affordance and constitutes its intentionality. An affordance is a property that is not only associated to us as living entities but is also connected to our skills to reply to that property. The embodied action inclinations involved in emotions can be defined as 'modes of bodily attunement' (Fuchs, 2013) that regulate the kind of admission we have to the object in question and the way we feel inspired to act towards it (Hufendiek, 2017).

The emotional affordance is key to understanding how materiality affect the practice of the users. This can be studied in the future, to understand how technology create a strong emotional attachment between users. Adapting digital settings to suit certain tasks for users who work frequently with technologies as a combined part of their work. This means that the emotional affordance of these digital environments is constituted by all the range of possible emotional states of their users. The affordance of technology must be extended to understand the ways in which people perceive, approach, and use technological artefacts. The achievements are not only related to the design characteristics of the devices, but also to the psychological and social characteristics of human-technology interaction. We suggest the term emotional affordance to better incorporate the emotional aspects of technological artefacts, keeping an eye on the qualities of technological environments to move towards more nuanced theories at the intersection of social processes and technological materiality.

References

Ahmed, S. (2010). *The Promise of Happiness*. Durham, NC: Duke University Press.

Belli, S. (2021). Affordance in socio-material networks: A mixed method study of researchers' groups and analog-digital objects. *Frontiers in Psychology*, 12, 1–13.

Benwell, B. and Stokoe, E. (2006). *Discourse and Identity*. Edinburgh: Edinburgh University Press.

Binkley, S. (2014). *Happiness as Enterprise. An Essay on Neoliberal Life*. New York: SUNY Press.

Bodtker, A.M., & Katz Jameson, J. (2001). Collective emotions in conflict situations: Societal implications. *International Journal of Conflict Management*, 12(3), 259–275. https://doi.org/10.1108/eb022858

Bootsma, R.J., Bakker, F.C., van Snippenberg, F.J. & Tdlohreg, C.W. (1992). The effects of anxiety on perceiving the reachability of passing objects. *Ecological Psychology*, 4, 1–16. https://doi.org/10.1080/10407413.1992.10530790

Brown, S., & Stenner, P. (2009). *Psychology without Foundations: History, Philosophy and Psychosocial Theory*. London: Sage.

Caltabiano, M.L. & Smithson, M. (1983). Variables affecting the perception of self-disclosure appropriateness. *The Journal of Social Psychology*, 120(1), 119–128.

Chaikin, A.L. & Derlega, V.J. (1974). Variables affecting the appropriateness of self-disclosure. *Journal of Consulting and Clinical Psychology*, 42(4), 588–593.

Chaudhuri, A., Aboulnasr, K., & Ligas, M. (2010). Emotional responses on initial exposure to a hedonic or utilitarian description of a radical innovation. *Journal of Marketing Theory and Practice*, 18, 339–359.

Clough, P. (2018). *The User Unconscious: On Affect, Media, and Measure*. Minneapolis: University of Minnesota Press.

Clough, P., & Willse, C. (2011). *Beyond Biopolitics: Essays on Governance of Life and Death*. Durham, NC: Duke University Press.

Colombetti, G. (2014). *The Feeling Body. Affective Science Meets the Enactive Mind*. Cambridge, MA: MIT Press.

Crider, J. & Ganesh, S. (2004). Negotiating meaning in virtual teams: Context, roles and computer-mediated communication in college classrooms. In: Godar, S.H. & Ferris, S.P. (eds), *Virtual and Collaborative Teams* (pp. 133–155). London: Idea Group.

Cromby, J. (2011). The greatest gift? Happiness, governance and psychology. *Social and Personality Psychology Compass*, 5(11), 840–852.

Darics, E., & Cristina Gatti, M. (2019). Talking a team into being in online workplace collaborations: The discourse of virtual work. *Discourse Studies*, 21(3), 237–257.

Davenport, S.W., Bergman, S.M., Bergman, J.Z., et al. (2014). Twitter versus Facebook: exploring the role of narcissism in the motives and usage of different social media platforms. *Computers in Human Behavior*, 32(1), 212–220.

Edwards, D. (1999). Emotion discourse. *Culture & Psychology*, 5(3), 271–291. https://doi.org/10.1177/1354067X9953001

Fox, J., Jones, E.B., & Lookadoo, K. (2013). *Romantic relationship dissolution on social networking sites: Social support, coping, and rituals on Facebook*. Paper presented at the 63rd Annual Conference of the International Communication Association, London, UK.

Fox, J., & Warber, K.M. (2014). Social networking sites in romantic relationships: Attachment, uncertainty, and partner surveillance on Facebook. *CyberPsychology, Behavior, and Social Networking*, 17, 3–7. http://dx.doi.org/10.1089/cyber.2012.0667

Fox, J., & Moreland, J.J. (2015). The dark side of social networking sites: An exploration of the relational and psychological stressors associated with Facebook use and affordances. *Computers in human behavior*, 45, 168–176.

Fuchs, T. (2013). The Phenomenology of Affectivity. In K. Fulford, et al. (eds.), *The Oxford Handbook of Philosophy and Psychiatry* (pp. 612–631). Oxford: Oxford University Press.

Gibson, J. (1986). *The Ecological Approach to Visual Perception*. New York: Psychology Press.

Graves, L. (2007). The affordances of blogging: A case study in culture and technological effects. *Journal of Communication Inquiry*, 31, 331–346. doi:10.1177/0196859907305446

Greco, M., & Stenner, P. (2013). Happiness and the art of life: Diagnosing the psychopolitics of wellbeing. *Health, Culture and Society*, 5(1), 1–19.

Hochschild, A. (2012). *The Outsourced Self: Intimate Life in Market Times*. New York, NY: Henry Holt.

Howell, A., & Conway, M. (1990). Perceived intimacy of expressed emotion. *The Journal of Social Psychology*, 130(4), 467–476.

Hufendiek, R. (2017). Affordances and the normativity of emotions. *Synthese*, 194(11), 4455–4476.

Hutchby, I. (2001). Technology, texts and affordances. *Sociology*, 35, 411–456.

Hutto, D. (2008). *Folk Psychological Narratives: The Sociocultural Basis of Understanding Reasons*. Cambridge, Mass.: MIT Press.

Illouz, E. (2008). *Cold Intimacies. The Making of Emotional Capitalism*. New York, NY: Polity.

Lapinski, M.K., & Rimal, R.N. (2005). An explication of social norms. *Communication Theory*, 15(2), 127–147.

Lara, A., Liu, W., Patrick Ashley, C., Nishida, A., Liebert, R., & Billies, M. (2017). Affect and subjectivity. *Subjectivity*, 10, 30–43.

Lara, A. (2020). *Decentering Subjectivity in Everyday Eating and Drinking: Digesting Reality*. London: Routledge.

Latour, B. (1999). Factures/fractures: From the concepts of the network to the concept of attachment. *Res: Anthropology & Aesthetics*, 36, 21–31.

Latour, B. (2004). How to talk about the body? The normative dimension of science studies. *Body & Society*, 10, 205–229.

Lim, Y. K., Donaldson, J., Jung, H., Kunz, B., Royer, D., Ramalingam, S., Thirumaran, S., & Stolterman, E. (2008). Emotional experience and interaction design. In C. Peter & R. Beale (eds.), *Affect and Emotion in Human-Computer Interaction: From Theory to Applications* (pp. 116–129). Berlin: Springer. https://doi.org/10.1007/978-3-540-85099-1_10

Lup, K., Trub, L., & Rosenthal, L. (2015). Instagram #Instasad?: Exploring associations among Instagram use, depressive symptoms, negative social comparison, and strangers followed. *Cyberpsychology, Behavior, and Social Networking*, 18(5), 247–252.

Maiese, M. (2011). *Embodiment, Emotion and Cognition*. Basingstoke: Palgrave Macmillan.

Marshall, T. C. (2012). Facebook surveillance of former romantic partners: Associations with postbreakup recovery and personal growth. *Cyberpsychology, Behavior, and Social Networking*, 15, 521–526. http://dx.doi.org/10.1089/cyber.2012.0125

Martínez-Guzmán, A., & Lara, A. (2019). Affective modulation in positive psychology's regime of happiness. *Theory & Psychology*, 29(3), 336–357.

Massumi, B. (2015). *Politics of Affect*. Malden, MA: Polity.

Meredith, J., & Stokoe, E. (2014). Repair: Comparing Facebook 'chat' with Spoken Interaction. *Discourse & Communication*, 8(2), 181–207. Https://Doi.Org/10.1177/1750481313510815

Mick, D. G., & Fournier, S. (1998). Paradoxes of technology: Consumer cognizance, emotions, and coping strategies. *Journal of Consumer Research*, 25, 123–143. https://doi.org/10.1086/209531

Nagy, P., & Neff, G. (2015). Imagined affordance: Reconstructing a keyword for communication theory. *Social Media+ Society*, 1(2), 2056305115603385.

Nass, C., & Moon, Y. (2000). Machines and mindlessness: Social responses to computers. *Journal of Social Issues*, 56, 81–103. https://doi.org/10.1111/0022-4537.00153

Neff, G., Jordan, T., McVeigh-Schultz, J., Gillespie, T. (2012). Affordances, technical agency, and the politics of technologies of cultural production. *Journal of Broadcasting & Electronic Media*, 56, 299–313. doi:10.1080/08838151.2012.678520

Newett, L., Churchill, B., & Robards, B. (2017). Forming connections in the digital era: Tinder, a new tool in young Australian intimate life. *Journal of Sociology*, 54(3), 346–361. https://doi.org/10.1177/1440783317728584

Norman, D. (1999). Affordances, constraints and design. *Interactions*, 6, 38–43. doi:10.1145/301153.301168

Parchoma, G. (2014). The contested ontology of affordances: Implications for researching technological affordances for collaborative knowledge production. *Computers in Human Behavior*, 37, 360–368.

Potter, J., & Hepburn, A. (2007). Discursive psychology: Mind and reality in practice. In *Language, Discourse and Social Psychology* (pp. 160–180). London: Palgrave Macmillan.

Prinz, J. J. (2007). Emotions, embodiment, and awareness. In L. Feldman Barrett, P. M. Niedenthal, & P. Winkielman (eds.), *Emotion and Consciousness* (pp. 363–383). New York: Guilford Press.

Protevi, J. (2009). *Political Affect: Connecting the Social and the Somatic*. Durham, NC: Duke University Press.

Przybylski, A. K., Murayama, K., DeHaan, C. R., & Gladwell, V. (2013). Motivational, emotional, and behavioral correlates of fear of missing out. *Computers in Human Behavior*, 29, 1841–1848. http://dx.doi.org/10.1016/j.chb.2013.02.014

Reeves, B., & Nass, C. (1996). *The Media Equation: How People Treat Computers, Television, and New Media Like Real People and Places*. New York: Cambridge University Press.

Saariluoma, P., & Jokinen, J. (2014). Emotional dimensions of user experience? A user psychological analysis. *International Journal of Human-Computer Interaction*, 30, 303–320. https://doi.org/10.1080/10447318.2013.858460

Sage, D., Vitry, C., & Dainty, A. (2019. Exploring the organizational proliferation of new technologies: An affective actor-network theory. *Organization Studies*, 41(3), 345–363.

Serrano-Pascual, A., & Carretero-García, C. (2022). Women's entrepreneurial subjectivity under scrutiny: Expert knowledge on gender and entrepreneurship. *Gender, Work & Organization*, 29(2), 666–686.

Sotgiu, I. (2013). *Psicologia della felicità e dell'infelicità* (Vol. 60). Rome: Carocci.

Thüring, M., & Mahlke, S. (2007). Usability, aesthetics and emotions in human–technology interaction. *International Journal of Psychology*, 42, 253–264. https://doi.org/10.1080/00207590701396674

Toma, C.L., & Hancock, J.T. (2013). Self-affirmation underlies Facebook use. *Personality and Social Psychology Bulletin*, 39, 321–331. http://dx.doi.org/ 10.1177/0146167212474694

Turkle, S. (2004). Whither psychoanalysis in computer culture? *Psychoanalytic Psychology*, 21, 16–30. https://doi.org/10.1037/0736-9735.21.1.16

Utz, S., & Beukeboom, C.J. (2011). The role of social network sites in romantic relationships: Effects on jealousy and relationship happiness. *Journal of Computer-Mediated Communication*, 16, 511–527. http://dx.doi.org/10.1111/ j.1083–6101.2011.01552.x

Waterloo, S., Baumgartner, S., Peter, J., & Valkenburg, P. (2017). Norms of online expressions of emotion: Comparing Facebook, Twitter, Instagram, and WhatsApp. *New Media & Society*, 20 (5), 1813–1831. doi: 10.1177/1461444817707349

Wood, S., & Moreau, P. (2006). From fear to loathing? How emotion influences the evaluation and early use of innovations. *Journal of Marketing*, 70(3), 44–57.

3
THE GAMIFICATION OF EMOTIONS
The digital turn

The digital turn has affected different areas of our lives, also modifying the way we interact and constituting new types of social relationship. In this third chapter, our interest is in the study of emotions in digital contexts, especially in the affective sphere and its variants. We claim that the contemporary society in which we live is based on social norms that privilege sharing well-being, happiness, and positive emotions and experiences, as we have seen at the end of the previous chapter. Social media is just a reflection of our society, and they ask us to follow exactly these same emotional patterns, as we will observe with different examples.

Along this chapter, emotions will assume a significant importance in the construction of social relationships and, moreover, in the processes of digital interactions between individuals, forming part of the social construction of their daily relationships. For example, love and happiness are just one of the many positive emotions that our social lives require us to share. From the moment that we try not to follow these rules, isolation, discomfort, and negative emotions occur. It is evident that there is less and less space in society to accept sad, rude, hostile, and angry individuals. On social media they are not given space either. It is something that in social psychology is defined with the principle of 'hedonic adaptation', which means that we perform the image of ourselves to our context. Nowadays, this means that it makes us feel good to be congratulated on our achievements in digital social networks, which, on the other hand, is something momentary and ephemeral.

Cabanas (2016) observed how in the last decade, neoliberal societies have witnessed a drastic 'happiness turn' (Ahmed, 2010), in which happiness has become ubiquitous, permeating every layer of the social realm. Happiness has become so widespread that it is no longer considered 'WEIRD' (western, educated, industrialized, rich, and democratic) (Henrich, Heine, & Norenzayan, 2010), but a psychological state that applies to all human beings equally. For example, Bergström

DOI: 10.4324/9781003247999-4

(2021) observed that digital technology like app and sites for dating, prove to be a stubbornly conventional invention, organized around the stereotypical opposition between sex (associated with men) and love (associated with women). The first ones look for casual sex, and the other for serious dating. Happiness has been established as a discourse that defines the norm of what is good, desirable, prosperous, and healthy in neoliberal societies. Layard claims that happiness must be considered 'the ultimate goal that enables us to judge other goals by how they contribute to it', a 'self-evident' good for all human beings, so a better society would be any society where the majority of individuals are either happy or pursue the achievement of happiness (Layard, 2005: 111). We will cover all these topics in this chapter.

3.1 The psychology of happiness

Ian Parker (2007), one of the most influential authors in the area of Critical Psychology, explains that 'Psychological theory is always a child of its time, and the theories do adapt and survive in the intellectual marketplace as the survival of the fittest ideas for capitalism' (p. 22). Psychology can be thought of as a disciplinary mechanism devoted to the production and regulation of the subject. It could be said that traditional models of psychology are specific expressions of current capitalism. Contemporary psychology, like positive psychology, work through the modulation of tendencies 'within the human' in contemporary capitalism (Martínez-Guzmán & Lara, 2019).

For Cabanas (2016), one of the main reasons accounting for the psychology of happiness stems from the fact that the discourse of happiness defines a model of selfhood that does not only align with the neoliberal ideology of individualism (Binkley, 2011; Davies, 2015; Honneth, 2004), but that also legitimizes and rekindles this ideology in seemingly nonideological terms through the discourse of science. The scientific study of happiness reveals that 90 per cent of human happiness depends upon individual psychological variables, so the role played by political, economic, and social aspects is, at most, secondary, either because they contribute very little, or because trying to influence or change those circumstances seems not to be worthwhile in terms of the individual's cost–benefit analysis of their personal well-being (Cabanas, 2016; Seligman, 2012). The outcome has been a widespread collapse of the social in favour of the psychological (Crespo & Freire, 2014) and with the discourse of personal happiness progressively substituting the discourse of individualism in the definition of the neoliberal model of citizenship (Cabanas, 2013, 2016; Cabanas & Huertas, 2014; Cabanas & Sánchez-González, 2012). The positive psychology is a branch of psychology that aims to study happiness and human well-being with scientific rigour, using a positivist framework (Martínez-Guzmán & Lara, 2019).

The critical analyses towards the psychology of 'happiness' have focused predominantly on the level of psychological individuality. This subjectification mode, based on self-regulation and the incessant capitalization of an individual's initiative, transcends the disciplinary mechanisms of the psy sciences, based on external normalization technologies, to move closer to the security mechanisms of neoliberal rationality (Martínez-Guzmán & Lara, 2019).

3.2 A new context for sharing emotions

Social media has been defined as 'sites and services that emerged in the early 2000s, including social media sites, video-sharing sites, blogs and microblogging platforms, and related tools that allow participants to create and share their own content' (Boyd, 2014: 6). In the last decade the use of these platforms has increased significantly. One of the reasons that explains the rise of these media is their pragmatic communicative potential, since they are defined as an important source of information for users (Aladwani & Dwivedi, 2018). It has been proven that the use of social networks facilitates the maintenance of relationships and can also increase sources of social support (McEwan, 2013; Nabi, Prestin, & So, 2013), which allows understanding the popularity among several generations. Some studies have shown that one reason why users spend many hours of their day using social platforms is to relax, entertain themselves or simply to interact with other people (Ku, Chu, & Tseng, 2013; Park, Kee, & Valenzuela, 2009). Beyond the benefits provided by the networks, some studies such as those by Chen & Lee (2013) have shown that social interaction through some platforms such as Facebook, are associated with a greater probability of suffering self-esteem and emotional security problems. These results agree with those found by Bevan, Gómez & Sparks (2014), who found a negative correlation between the time spent on social networks and the quality of life experienced. Or what is the same, less use of social networks seems to be associated with enjoying greater well-being (Hinsch & Sheldon, 2013).

These social platforms can be used for multiple purposes, including emotional regulation. A series of investigations carried out through content analysis have shown that the publications shared publicly in these cybernetic spaces have a high load of emotional content (Kivran-Swaine & Naaman, 2011; Kramer, Guillory, & Hancock, 2014), which is attractive from the psychological point of view. Despite the small scientific production in the field of emotions shared on social networks, there is data that suggests that nine out of ten emotional experiences are shared on some digital platform. Following this line, scientific research has identified a positive bias in publications, that is, there is a preference on the part of users to share materials with a positive charge on the web (Reinecke & Trepte, 2014). With the increasing acceptance of websites, in which direct contact does not intervene, the need to present yourself to the general public in a positive way to make a good impression seems immutable. Users need the approval of others to feel socially accepted, a fact that leads them to act in different ways outside the social norms of the physical world. This peculiarity of publications finds its explanation in the social norms that govern online activity.

Among the multiple risks detected, in a large number of studies, are social rejection, disapproval or betrayal of others (Greene, Derlega & Mathews, 2006), and the probability of acquiring a negative public image (Leary & Kowalski, 1990).

Therefore, studying precautionary norms is particularly important to understand self-expressive behaviours in these parts (Waterloo, Baumgartner, Peter, & Valkenburg, 2017). Since not all platforms are configured with the same dynamics, the nature of the publications may vary depending on the place of publication (Uski & Lampinen, 2016). The control exercised by the configurations of social platforms encourages users to present themselves in publicly well-viewed and accepted ways, therefore both the nature of the social network and the intrinsic norms of relationships, where human beings play a mediating role in uploading the content to be shared.

Many social networks invite users to share emotions, encouraging them to constantly update their thoughts, feelings and personal experiences (Derks, Fischer & Bos, 2008). Although there is not much empirical evidence on the nature of the norms that regulate self-expression in networks, some studies agree on the tendency of people to publish both positive and negative emotions, although with a slight tendency to show themselves favourably (Lin, Tov & Oiu, 2014). The existence of this positive bias could be explained by the favourability norms that social networks promote (Reinecke & Trepte, 2014). In the same way, some authors attribute the cause of this characteristic to showing positive feelings more frequently to social desirability (Caltabiano & Smithson, 1983).

As for the other side of the coin, it would seem that the public disclosure of negative emotions could be perceived as strange behaviours that are not very adaptive to the presentation of unknown users (Chaikin & Derlega, 1974), so that the social image of the person could be compromised. On the contrary, Rose (2002) understands that the expression of negative emotions online can favour the establishment of intimate social connections, since research on co-rumination indicates that sharing negative experiences could strengthen relational ties (Rose, 2002).

3.3 The gamification of our emotions

> Our mission is to create new connections and bring the world closer together and help people meet others they otherwise wouldn't have met.
>
> *Tinder, February 2017*

In this section, we show how the digital transformation of our emotions has assumed levels of gamification that allow us to interact and get excited without having to make a lot of effort. New digital environments stimulate opening minds in the selection of possible romantic partners and allow different emotional connections with potential partners. Platforms such as Tinder and Grindr have allowed this step, removing the stress the physical and emotional exhaustion that existed in the analogue world to meet these potential partners. This is the seduction of the game, which allows us to enter into emotional practices with minimal physical and emotional exhaustion. Obviously, this gamification has emotional consequences in people's lives. We can of course understand that this game becomes real when the emotions that appear in these practices affect our bodies and our lives.

As Alessandro Baricco (2019) mentions, this digital transformation of our lives has assumed levels of gamification that allow us to interact and get excited without having to make a lot of effort. New digital environments stimulate opening minds in the selection of possible romantic partners and allow different emotional connections with potential partners (Gibbs, Ellison & Lai, 2011; Sprecher, 2009). The internet has a profound impact upon the extent and nature of romantic and sexual relationship (Ben-Ze'ev, 2004). This gamification is fast and liquid and is distributed in networks of romantic possibilities, to quote Zygmunt Bauman (2003). Subjects connected to these platforms wonder why we should try to approach strangers in a public space such as in a bar when it is cold and raining outside and our bodies are exhausted from our work day. On the other hand, being quietly in a protected environment such as the sofa at home, we can meet many more single people and interact with them at the same time in total safety. This is the seduction of the game, which allows us to enter into emotional practices with minimal physical effort. Users of these platforms prefer the efficiency and security that these social networks offer (Hobbs et al., 2017).

Online dating makes everything go faster, that's what users say (Bergström, 2021). Contacting or responding to someone is immediately understood as a sign of sexual interest. The ambiguity that often characterizes other social interactions is completely absent: the only reason for two people to communicate is to assess each other as potential partners. Online dating is less consequential than ordinary dating (Bergström, 2021). Online dating has made self-governance the primary mode of control of contemporary sexualities. As Bergström (2021) explains, online dating is a way for young, and not so young, people to see how well they measure up to conventional female and male norms, like a game. On dating platforms young people have the opportunity to flirt without anyone watching and to converse with and meet people new to them, whom they may not have dared to approach in other circumstances and whom they do not have to again if they do not want to (Bergström, 2021). Illouz (2012) sees a free market of sexual encounters that has given rise to a new form of emotional domination of women by men, expressed in women's emotional availability, and men's reluctance to commit to women, because the conditions of choice have changed. The main idea is that men are more inclined to have casual sex and women more inclined to have a relationship (Bergström, 2021). Dating apps stand accused of making sex too easy and of serving men's interests. Glued to their mobile phones and hooked on Netflix, internet porn, or dating apps, the generations born in and after the 1990s are supposedly incapable of and uninterested in creating physical connections in real life (Twenge, 2017).

Bergström (2021) suggests that the new sexual norms, together with the new technology, have made young people, a 'Tinder generation', unwilling to commit or incapable of commitment; they cast aside love and embrace casual sex instead, a sort of banalization of sex, as mundane as any leisure activity. Digital dating as a commodification of intimate relationships brings economic logic into the sphere of intimacy because dating platforms are structured as a market, governed by competition, self-marketing, and choice strategies. Illouz denounces the penetration of the capitalist cultural grammar into heterosexual romantic relationship (Illouz, 2012). Romantic encounters have the principles of mass consumption based on an economy of abundance, endless choice, efficiency, rationalization, selective targeting, and standardization (Illouz, 2007). A significant proportion of today's couples meet through online dating (Cacioppo et al., 2013). These platforms stand accused of turning users into consumers incapable of committing to one person. Online dating is radically different from meeting at a club or in a bar because the platforms are accessible from home, and hence they turn meeting a partner into a domestic activity. Second, far from having a public setting, interactions are strictly dyadic, being based on one-to-one conversations that cannot be seen or overhead by a third part.

Obviously, this gamification has emotional consequences in people's lives. In romantic relationships, what Bauman (2003) identifies as liquid love is taking place, which allows a number of hypothetical relationships that affect other types of relationships, perhaps more stable and lasting (Barraket & Henry-Waring, 2008; Couch & Liamputtong, 2008; Goluboff, 2015; Jacobsen, 2019). The concept of 'networked individualism' (Rainie & Wellman, 2012) is easily applicable in the practices of the users of these social networks, that is, connected individuals who have access to a vast network of romantic possibilities. This 'network of intimacy' is what Giddens calls 'plastic sexuality' (Giddens, 1991), which allows a flirtation and an experience of love and fulfilment that brings new freedoms, opportunities, and pleasures, but also old and new anxieties about risks, self-image and love (Hobbs et al., 2017). We can of course understand that this game becomes real when the emotions that appear in these practices affect our bodies and our lives. Online relationships are conducted between actual, flesh-and-blood people (Ben-Ze'ev, 2004). The flirtation that started while watching a series on Netflix while sitting comfortably on the sofa at home is no longer a game when the person with whom you are chatting is no longer behind a screen but in front of us and materializes in a real body.

Santos Ortega, Serrano-Pascual & Borges (2021) present us with a quantified self that makes it possible to make the subject intelligible, calculable, comparable, and makes it possible to rank personal performance. The quantified self is related to other terms and currents such as body-hacking. Self-assessment methods present in fields as diverse as the cultural industry (self-application test) or therapeutic intervention (methods of recording manifestations of suffering in the body, mind, emotions) (Allard-Poesi & Hollet-Haudebert, 2012). In short, they would be technologies that allow practices to be tracked and made visible to make them more manageable and predictable. (Un)employment, inequality, health, well-being, happiness, are no longer represented in a collective code to be understood as the responsibility of the individual. Practices of a very diverse nature, such as programmes to combat dependence on the unemployed (employment activation), the transformation of political rationalities in the government of old age ('active ageing'), the industry of happiness (Cabanas e Illouz, 2019), converge in promoting a process of incorporating the metaphor of the company, and its underlying values, as a framework of meaning, restricting intersubjective awareness and weakening collective subjects (Santos Ortega, Serrano-Pascual & Borges, 2021). In this sense, the demand for emotional self-regulation stands out as a priority social demand, as well as one of the key elements that motivate consumption. Eva Illouz (2007, 2008), for example, has coined the term 'emotional capitalism' to show the intimate relationship between the demand for emotional self-control and the logic of consumption in advanced capitalist societies (Cabanas, 2016).

It has also been observed how digital transformation becomes a potential source for frustration and anxiety when users of these technologies do not have an expected response (Ceaparu, Lazar, Bessiere, Robinson & Shneiderman, 2004; Jokinen, 2015). In the same way that the possibilities of positive emotions multiply, the possibilities of negative emotions also multiply (Hadlington & Scase, 2018). The frustration for something expected and that has not arrived, or for the continuous wait, which anticipates a possible failure, would be an example. This continuous 'state of tension' does not allow a healthy emotional balance for the individual. For this reason, many prefer not to be connected, partially due to frustrating experiences (Zickuhr, 2013). Other users, on the other hand, have experienced a form of dependence on these technologies, and for this reason they have preferred to disconnect (Paasonen, 2015).

For Newett, Churchill & Robards (2018), having a greater number of connections does not mean having more connection, that is, the quantity is not related to the quality of the relationship with our contacts. In their research, many of the users claim that even though they have multiple suitors for a potential date, they question the genuineness of these relationships. For this reason, many of the relationships that are born in these platforms are considered less legitimate and 'natural' than the relationships that are generated in the face-to-face (Newett et al., 2018).

The impact that these digital practices produce on social dynamics in terms of inclusion or exclusion and their effects on the processes of construction of virtual social identities interests us not only as users in the first person, but also because of the opening of horizons that they imply within the study of human relationships. The difficulty of a user inhabiting a digital space correctly and the discomfort caused by the feeling of inadequacy, often give rise to feelings of anger, frustration, rage, or fear. The fear of sharing a digital space that is not known perfectly or the fear of relating to the digital community produces discomfort and misunderstandings in human relationships. Many users decide to disappear from these networks, committing suicide their online identities after seeing that there is no worthy future for them in these worlds (Belli & De Eugenio, 2014).

3.4 Emotions in social networks

Every year several new social networks appears in our digital lives. Each social platform represents a unique social context (Marwick & Boyd, 2011). Theoretically, the differences in the technical characteristics and the unique context that each network offers should be accompanied by a change in the prevailing norms, and consequently in the shared content (Postmes, Spears & Lea, 2000).

To facilitate the analysis of the messages shared on social networks, use can be made of the identification of three characteristics that allow defining the specific social context provided by a platform, which includes: the behaviour privacy settings, its monitoring mechanism, and the modality (Waterloo, Baumgartner, Peter, & Valkenburg, 2017). Behavioural privacy is defined as the way in which behaviour is expressed in a specific context, whether it is public or private (Lapinski & Rimal, 2005). Closely related to this first feature, the tracking mechanism appears. This occurs when the user must accept the request received in order to establish a link with the interested party. Follow-up can be reciprocal or non-reciprocal. The reciprocal mechanism is defined when both agents accept the request sent by the other party, allowing them to freely exchange publications without restrictions. Non-reciprocal tracking, on the other hand, allows the issuing user to follow another without the latter having to forcibly follow them (Lup, Trub & Rosenthal, 2015). This characteristic is typical of the configurative mechanism of Twitter, in which users can follow others without the need for approval or reciprocity. Finally, modality occupies an important role in the defining configuration of the platform. This property defines the type of content that can be shared on the networks. In the case of Facebook and Twitter, the platforms allow both textual and visual content to be shared, in addition to attaching links to other external platforms. On the contrary, Instagram is a platform designed to share visual content with a wide range of filters to retouch the material that you want to publish. The possibility of being able to alter the images and share them publicly, makes Instagram a widely used tool among young people to promote their image in a socially acceptable way (Sheldon & Bryant, 2016).

The nature of the public that makes up the network is also a variable to take into account when deciding on a particular means of communication. As Waterloo, Baumgartner, Peter and Valkenburg (2017) have shown in their research, the social network WhatsApp is used mainly to interact with people who are part of close ties, unlike Twitter, which revolves more around communication with people with weak ties (Karapanos, Teixeira & Gouveia, 2016). The fact of being able to follow any other user without the need for their approval, beyond the possible benefits, makes Twitter a less secure tool due to the possibility of incursion by strange users (Lin, Tov & Oiu, 2014).

Regardless of the networks used, the knowledge produced in the new lines of research suggests that publicly shared emotions are less intense than those expressed in intimacy (Bazarova, Choi, Sosik, Cosley & Whitlock, 2015). Trust and bond with the receiver are a very important piece when determining the intensity of the content. In general, there seems to be a consensus within the framework of the research on the nature of the network and the magnitude of the shared message. People are more likely to disclose personal information with strong ties than with people with whom there is not such a close relationship (Karapanos, Teixeira & Gouveia, 2016). Similarly, the evidence found suggests that the use of private communication channels, such as WhatsApp, is more likely in the interaction with people with whom a close bond is maintained than with people with whom there are weak ties (Haythornthwaite, 2005). In this way, the use of Twitter and Instagram, both supported by non-reciprocal following, is associated with interaction with weak ties and the greater probability of interacting with people outside the proximity circle (Lup, Trub & Rosenthal, 2015).

Currently Twitter stands out as one of the most used social platforms with about 330 million active users per month (Statista, 2019). The defining characteristic of this social platform is the limitation of messages to 140 characters (Martínez, Martín, Ureña & Montejo, 2012; Szto & Gray, 2015; Thornton, 2013), which allows users to share thoughts and express emotions in real time (Allsop, Basset & Hoskins, 2007), without the need for delay. The disposition and pragmatism of the commands makes Twitter a simple and very intuitive network, accessible to any user regardless of age (Taddicken, 2014).

The increase in the use of Twitter in recent years does not fall solely on personal use. As collected by Barnes & Mattson (2009) in their study in which they analyzed the activity of more than 500 companies, 52 per cent of the companies confessed to using Twitter, and 82 per cent of them reported it being a success. In the business field, several inquiries have been made to capture the emotional reactions of users through digital platforms, and more recently on Twitter (Rathore & Ilavarasan, 2018). As Jansen, Zhang, Sobel & Chowdury (2009) point out, about a quarter of the analyzed tweets referred to a commercial brand. This act by users of communicating something about a product, initiates the co-creation process. The analysis of the emotions evoked by a new product makes it easier for the creative company to predict the success of the evaluated good (Jeong, Yoon, & Lee, 2017; Shirdastian, Laroche & Richard, 2017). Moreover, by launching new products on social networks, companies manage to connect emotionally with users responding to commercial purposes. The presence of propaganda activities based on sentimental stimulation opens up new paradigms in the analysis of publications and commerce.

Many of the studies carried out so far have concentrated their efforts on analyzing the functionality of social networks in specific theoretical contexts. Despite the fullness experienced in all areas, the causes that motivate the choice of a particular social platform are still unknown. A first explanatory approach to the question of choice lies in the affordance provided by each network (Choi & Toma, 2014; Helles, 2013). 'The affordances of a digital medium refer to the subjective perceptions of the digital object's utility that arise out of its objective qualities' (Vanden Abeele, Schouten & Antheunis, 2016: 2). That is, the possibilities perceived by the subject to communicate their emotional experiences within a digital environment. When a tweet is published, it has the possibility of being replicated by another user. Similarly, an account holder can mention another in a publication, which is known as a Twitter 'handle' (Dwyer & Fraser, 2016). Marvick & Boyd (2011) have described the audience, the actual and potential viewers of tweets, as 'networked public'. The audience plays an important role in the act, those to whom the message is directed – defines the social context of interaction (Boyd, 2014), so its content is determined in part by this audience that participates in the publications.

Since its inception in 2007, Twitter users have made use of hashtags in their messages. The incorporation of the hashtag sign (#) accompanied by a word allows adding all the tweets on a particular topic in a list available in the Twitter search function (Weller, Bruns, Burgess, Mahrt, & Cornelius, 2014). This exercise makes it possible to monitor all the tweets tagged with this expression, regardless of the networks of users' followers, and facilitates the visibility and expansiveness of the publications in the digital context (Weller, Bruns, Burgess, Mahrt & Cornelius, 2014). Easy access to the multiple realities shared on Twitter offers the possibility of interacting in a new non-physical context, in which both the norms and patterns of interaction break with traditional perspectives of the physical world. However, the publications shared in the digital context provide the consequences arising in a specific environment and allow users to enter a specific time and space without the need to have experienced the situation in the first person.

Research on Twitter covers a vast range of disciplines and pursues a wide range of different objectives. In its beginnings, the studies of Twitter publications were promoted from the field of linguistics, driven by the need to understand the meaning and structure of texts in the new contexts of digital action (Biber, Conrad & Reppen, 1998). More recently, new disciplines such as marketing or psychology have begun to show interest in analyzing publications with the aim of conceiving how people think and feel in relation to a product or a given situation (Pennebaker, Mehl & Niederhoffer, 2003). A study carried out by Dhiraj & Longwell (2012), demonstrated the high influence capacity of Twitter, raising the technical scientific importance of the network to another level. Specifically, the researchers tracked and examined posts during the 2010 Pakistan floods and realized the communicative potential of messages shared online.

To date, much of the research on the use of emotions and new technologies, and specifically on Twitter, leads to a predominance of the publication of messages containing positive emotions, such as surprise and happiness. The dissemination of affective content on social platforms is mainly associated with informative purposes, either to sell or to maintain contact with followers (Sohn, 2014). The preponderance of tweets associated with negative emotions such as fear and anger, serve a dual purpose. On the one hand, the dissemination of negative emotions in the forum of the social network has made it possible to represent in a virtual environment, cognitive and affective reactions of users to unpleasant political and social events in the physical world. And on the other, and in line with the findings of Radcliffe, Lumley, Kendall, Stevenson & Beltran (2010), the propagation of sensory reactions with other users would fulfil a biological function. From what we know from some recent studies in the field of clinical psychology, openly demonstrating the emotional state with other users leads to an increase in the feeling of well-being and reduces the presence of anxiety-depressive symptoms (Langens, 2005).

In the field of emotions, the research is still in its preliminary stages. However, the analysis and detection of affective components is not entirely uninhibited. The methodologies used in the pioneering studies have been fundamentally: linguistic analysis, social analysis, content analysis and discourse analysis (Eysenbach, 2011;

Paul & Dredze, 2011; Rentschler, 2015) to predict and find out future behaviours. Similarly, some investigations such as those by Chen and Lee (2013), interested in exclusively analyzing the emotional component of social networks, have based their analyses on more complex models such as the linguistic method of natural language processing (Desmet & Hoste, 2013), or reasoning based on cases (Kao et al., 2009).

An example of the growing interest on the part of the scientific community in the analysis of messages published in the digital context, and specifically on Twitter, is demonstrated by the large number of tools that have been designed to collect and generate virtual databases. Methods focused on the lexical component, for example, make use of an emotional vocabulary to detect a specific emotion in the text (Joshi et al., 2016). Learning methods, meanwhile, contemplate both supervised learning, and unsupervised in order to detect emotions using various classification and grouping methods (Mohammad & Kiritchenko, 2015). More recently, statistical models such as the Naïve Bayes algorithm are being incorporated to classify tweets directly with the sentiment and emotion contained in the message (Sailunaz & Alhajj, 2019).

The EMOTEX model is another example of the great appeal that digital platforms have awakened. Specifically, this model allows classifying large amounts of text with little effort (Hasan, Rundensteiner & Agu, 2014). Similarly, the T-PIECE model developed by Kafeza and colleagues (2014) enables researchers to identify the most influential users by classifying them in a personality cluster based on the tweets shared on a specific topic.

The increasing popularity of social networks and the importance of emotions in the lives of human beings, lead us to wonder what role the digital platform Twitter plays in regulating the affective component in people's daily lives. In the same way, it is of interest to us to analyze how emotions are expressed and how experiences that occur in the 'real' context are shared to the digital context. For this, emotions considered basic have been used for a matter of empirical pragmatism and accessibility. However, we acknowledge the point at which research in the field of emotions is at and we validate the naturalistic and experimental studies that demonstrate the importance of the socio-historical factor and the personal character of affective reactions. In a second point, it is intended to evaluate how the affective reactions that occur in a given context are transferred and shared to the digital space.

3.5 Towards a hybrid theory?

Thus, emotions are defined and evolve thanks to language, being continuously in process. Although the context in which they generate and express is the image, they continue to maintain a close dependence on the verbal dimension, both in the interpretation of images and in the recognition of emotions, it is the experience and communication to others of the same. The image requires a symbolic context to be effective, it is always inserted in a broader frame of reference that gives it its meaning and above all allows it to establish its authenticity and credibility. In this sense, the interpretation that usually accompanies the image and its interpretive insertion in a historical context that facilitates whoever emits them is fundamental in the generation of emotions. In the same way, with the arrival of the so-called digital transformation in our daily and professional practices, emotions follow this transformation process, or at least the way we refer to them through language. When our emotions are associated with digital technologies, these online spaces are directly connected with the analogue space (Jurgenson, 2012), since what happens and is expressed in the online world we also feel in the offline world. The process of testing emotions in different spaces makes the analogue body the only recipient of these emotions in the end, since all these different emotions will always pass through there. For this reason, Jurgenson (2012) is critical in how the discussion between online and offline spaces is generated, reinforcing this dichotomy when the separation of these spaces is futile. The author introduces the term digital dualism to criticize this separation and focuses on the interaction of these two interconnected spaces. According to him, these spaces are so close together that a division between online and offline space is unproductive and perpetuates claims that the emotions experienced in digital contexts are less real than those experienced in analogue contexts.

This is an issue that can be influenced by a hybrid theory (Belli, Aceros, Harré, 2015). This approach recognizes a three-fold set of conditions of emotion: a physiological component, a cognitive component, and a social component. As a result, the complexity of the study of emotions becomes evident. This complexity can increase if we consider the current contexts in which emotions are socially displayed. In recent years, online communication and the internet have probably introduced a different grammar of emotion, a new emo-grammar where researchers return to discover the important role of emotions in communication between users. Probably the complexity of emotions is represented by the complexity of the language in this online communication where users don't use body and facial strategies to express them. Do not forget the vast increase in video presentations – a new iconography of emotions must surely be the focus of new studies. We have extensions of discourse also in Twitter, and other instant responses and displays. But the most important is the pictorial content of Facebook and similar social networks, with the ever-present possibility of recording how someone looks at a precise moment.

McLuhan (1964) teaches us that the medium is the message, that is to say that one of the most important characteristics of the media we use to communicate, in this case the digital space of social interaction, is its ability to modify the course and the functioning of human relationships and, consequently, our emotions (Ansari, 2015; Hobbs, Owen & Gerber, 2017; Slater, 2013). Interest in the study of emotions in digital contexts has specialized especially in the affective sphere and its variants. We cannot argue that the contemporary society in which we live is based on social norms that privilege sharing well-being, positivity, and our social experiences. Social media is just a reflection of our society, and they ask us to follow exactly these same emotional patterns.

In the area of ethnomethodology and conversational analysis, it has been observed how online interactions have been enriched by different ways of representing the emotional experience in their conversations. For example, emoticons – combinations of punctuation marks used to convey facial expressions (Benwell & Stokoe, 2010). These signs became 'smileys', images that reflect these emoticons, and now there is a wide range of 'emojis' that can indicate the mood or posture of a speaker at a particular moment of the interaction. From a conversational analysis perspective, emoticons are generally understood depending on the sequential and interactional context in which they are used (Markman & Oshima, 2007; Meredith & Stokoe, 2014). For example, emojis shared at the beginning of a shift indicate a posture towards the previous shift, while an emoji posted at the end of a shift indicates a posture towards the shift itself, providing information to the recipient on how it should be understood (Meredith & Stokoe, 2014). Despite the etymology of emoticons (a combination of emotion and icon), it has been shown that emoticons are not only used to convey emotional content in digital settings, but are used more consciously than non-verbal behaviour (Derks, Bos, von Grumbkow, 2007; Sampietro, 2016; Yus, 2014). One of the functions that researchers clearly recognize is the signalling of irony or jokes in their conversations (Dresner & Herring, 2010; Yus, 2014). Several researchers have also linked the use of emoticons with discursive strategies, as they can be used to soften or tone threatening formulations (Calero Vaquera, 2014; Wilson, 1993) and as positive markers of courtesy (Kavanagh, 2010; Skovholt, Grønning & Kankaanranta, 2014; Vandergriff, 2013). In daily interactions in the workplace, Darics and Gatti (2012) found that emoticons were used primarily to mitigate or clarify the message for the purpose of successful peer cooperation. As the literature review shows, there is evidence that indicates that emojis not only communicate affection but also improve the written text that they accompany (Sampietro, 2019).

Emojis allow us to share and negotiate emotions in digital contexts to try not to exercise exclusionary practices and socio-digital discrimination. In these contexts, Hobbs & colleagues (2016) confirm that shared emotions affect both relationships in the offline world and in the online world. For this reason, they mention that shared emotions in the online world are healthy as long as this practice is moderate and complemented by offline interactions. Instead, negative dynamics occur when the emotions expressed are limited to the online world in their extreme case. These digital spaces are understood as a 'Now' and a 'Here', determined by our time and space, which we occupy when we share emotions through an intimate space made up of our bodies and screens.

This digital turn also considers the fact that emotions originate in the course of digital interactions and play an important role in the construction, maintenance and transformation of social order (Guedes & Álvaro, 2010). These socialization processes are possible because they are closely related to the expression of emotions (Turner & Stets, 2004). According to Guedes & Álvaro (2010), emotions have a significant importance in the construction of social relationships and, therefore, in the processes of digital interactions between individuals, forming part of the social construction of their daily relationships. It is evident that, if our lives are only based on this emotional support that the networks provide us, in the end we are left with a great emptiness and a feeling of loneliness. Taquet & colleagues (2016) indicate that when people are happy and satisfied with their lives, they do not have the need to do activities that make them feel better and, of course, to share them. Those who post photos of a party with friends from the night before, according to the study, belong to someone who is in a situation where he misses these positive emotions because he is actually unhappy and dissatisfied with his life. According to the study authors, our positive emotions can be considered as a resource. We are going to use them when we need them to feel better, so photos of these experiences are published to receive 'likes' among our friends and followers, and in this way feedback these positive emotions that are absent.

3.6 Conclusion

In this chapter, we have presented recent scientific contributions in the field of social psychology of emotions and the impact they have had in different places. It is evident that the study of emotions is even more complex if we consider the digital turn that this line of research has had in recent years. In the so-called digital turn, we have been able to observe how in recent years online communication has introduced a different grammar of emotions, that is, a new emo-grammar (Belli, Aceros & Harré, 2015), where researchers rediscover the important role that emotions play in communication between users who share the same 'emotional dictionary' (Hochschild, 2019). Probably in this context the density of emotions is represented by the complexity of the language used in this online communication, a communication for which users do not use body language or facial strategies to express themselves. We must be prepared as researchers in the field of emotions, that due to the great increase in these digital tools, a new graphic representation of emotions, with great security, will be the focus of new studies in the coming decades. However, we have observed how the most elementary thing in these new contexts is emotional expression, and therefore one of the great challenges for the future will be to develop a methodology to monitor the constant possibility of recording the way in which these emotions arise in a precise moment.

In the 21st century, digital platforms such as Twitter have embraced a dimension other than the initial one; they represent and transform social acts. Discursive psychology as a method is a good ally to decipher the codes of the new reality. Emotions continue to maintain gaps in the innate and universal paradigms, but the differences found in the categorization process reinforce the idea that supports the pedagogical influence of the cultural factor, even intrapersonal. Disseminating personal experiences or sharing cognitions regarding the same event are stimuli that reinforce the construction of the network, and transform the identity of the person (Wittgenstein, 1958). The messages shared in the forum fulfil many different linguistic functions, which generate an impact on personal cognitions, reinforcing in the new contexts the idea of 'perlocutionary act' of Austin (1955), according to which the fact of communicating something simple as it may be, implicitly entails a set of changes and consequences in the thoughts and emotions of the receiving agents. Throughout this chapter, we have observed how the performance of emotions, that is, the expression, intensity, and manifestations of these, are transformed over time and across cultures through our discursive productions. Extending the invitation of Hochschild (2019), we share that the feeling that emotions are 'out there', from the global mobilizations against climate change to the transnational journeys of refugees, war conflicts, and catastrophes. These are different stories and narratives that are worth studying to understand what problems and questions the study of emotions should find answers to.

References

Ahmed, S. (2010). *The Promise of Happiness*. Durham, NC: Duke University Press.

Aladwani, A.M., & Dwivedi, Y.K. (2018). Towards a theory of socio citizenry: Quality anticipation, trust configuration, and approved adaptation of governmental social media. *International Journal of Information Management*, 43, 261–272. doi: 10.1016/j.ijinfomgt.2018.08.009

Allard-Poesi, F., & Hollet-Haudebert, S. (2012). La construction du sujet souffrant au travail au travers des instruments scientifiques de mesure. *@GRH*, 4(5), 45–74.

Allsop, D., Basset, B., & Hoskins, J. (2007). Word-of-mouth research: Principles and applications. *Journal of Advertising Research*, 47(4), 398–411. doi: 10.2501/S0021849907070419

Ansari, A. (2015). *Modern Romance*. London: Allen Lane.

Austin, J. (1955 (1998)). *How to Do Things with Words*. Cambridge: Cambridge University Press.

Baricco, A. (2019). *The Game*. Barcelona: Anagrama.

Barnes, N.G., & Mattson, E. (2009). *US charities' adoption of social media outpaces all other sectors for the third year in a row*. Retrieved from the University of Massachusetts Dartmouth Center for Marketing Research website: www.fcae.umassd.edu/cmr/studiesresearch/charitystudy.cfm

Barraket, J., & Henry-Waring, M.S. (2008). Getting it on(line): Sociological perspectives on E-dating. *Journal of Sociology*, 44(2), 149–165. https://doi.org/10.1177/1440783308089167

Bauman, Z. (2003). *Liquid Love: On the Frailty of Human Bonds*. Cambridge: Polity.

Bazarova, N.N., Choi, Y.H., Schwanda Sosik, V., Cosley, D., & Whitlock, J. (2015). Social sharing of emotions on Facebook: Channel differences, satisfaction, and replies. Paper presented at CSCW 2015. Vancouver, Canada.

Belli, S., Aceros, J., & Harré, R. (2015). 'It's all discursive!' Crossing boundaries and crossing words with Rom Harré. *Universitas Psychologica*, 14(2), 771–784. https://doi.org/10.11144/Javeriana.upsy14-2.iadc

Belli, S., & De Eugenio, G. (2014). Prácticas emocionales y procesos subjetivadores en la sociedad digital: el caso de los suicidios online. *Quaderns de Psicología*, 16(2), 57–72. https://doi.org/10.5565/rev/qpsicologia.1181

Benwell, B., & Stokoe, E. (2010). Analysing identity in interaction: Contrasting discourse, genealogical, narrative and conversation analysis. In M. Wetherell & C.T. Mohanty, *The SAGE Handbook of Identities* (pp. 82–103). London: SAGE Publications. https://doi.org/10.4135/9781446200889.n6

Ben-Ze'ev, A. (2004). *Love Online: Emotions on the Internet*. Cambridge: Cambridge University Press.

Bergström, M. (2021). *The New Laws of Love: Online Dating and the Privatization of Intimacy.* Cambridge: John Wiley & Sons.

Bevan, J.L., Gomez, R., & Sparks, L. (2014). Disclosures about important life events on Facebook: Relationships with stress and quality of life. *Computers in Human Behavior,* 39, 246–253. https://doi.org/10.1016/j.chb.2014.07.021

Biber, D., Conrad, S., & Reppen, R. (1998). *Corpus Linguistics: Investigating Language Structure and Use.* New York: Cambridge University Press.

Binkley, S. (2011). Happiness, positive psychology and the program of neoliberal governmentality. *Subjectivity,* 4(4), 371–394.

Boyd, D. (2014). *It's complicated: The social lives of networked teens.* New Haven, CT: Yale University Press

Cabanas, E. (2013). *La felicidad como imperativo moral: origen y difusión del individualismo 'positivo' y sus efectos en la construcción de la subjetividad (doctoral dissertation).* Universidad Auónoma de Madrid, Madrid.

Cabanas, E. (2016). Rekindling individualism, consuming emotions: Constructing 'psytizens' in the age of happiness. *Culture & Psychology,* 22(3), 467–480.

Cabanas, E., & Huertas, J.A. (2014). Psicología positiva y psicología popular de la autoayuda: Un romance histórico, psicológico y popular. *Anales de Psicología,* 30(3), 852–864.

Cabanas, E., & Illouz, E. (2019). *Happycracia: cómo la ciencia y la industria de la felicidad controlan nuestras vidas.* Paidós Ibérica: Madrid.

Cabanas, E., & Sánchez-González, J.C. (2012). The roots of positive psychology. *Papeles Del Psicólogo,* 33(3), 172–182.

Cacioppo, J.T., Cacioppo, S., Gonzaga, G.C., Ogburn, E.L., & VanderWeele, T.J. (2013). Marital satisfaction and break-ups differ across on-line and off-line meeting venues. *Proceedings of the National Academy of Sciences,* 110(25), 10135–10140.

Calero Vaquera, L.M. (2014). El discurso del WhatsApp: entre el Messenger y el SMS. *Oralia,* 17, 85–114.

Caltabiano, M.L., & Smithson, M. (1983). Variables affecting the perception of self-disclosure appropriateness. *The Journal of Social Psychology,* 120(1): 119–128.

Ceaparu, I., Lazar, J., Bessiere, K., Robinson, J., & Shneiderman, B. (2004). Determining causes and severity of end-user frustration. *International Journal of Human-Computer Interaction,* 17(3), 333–356. https://doi.org/10.1207/s15327590ijhc1703_3

Chaikin, A.L. & Derlega, V.J. (1974). Variables affecting the appropriateness of self-disclosure. *Journal of Consulting and Clinical Psychology* 42(4): 588–593.

Chen, W., & Lee, K. (2013). Sharing, liking, commenting, and distressed? The pathway between Facebook interaction and psychological distress. *Cyberpsychology, Behavior, and Social Networking,* 16, 728–734. doi: 10.1089/cyber.2012.0272

Choi, M., & Toma, C.L. (2014). Social sharing through interpersonal media: Patterns and effects on emotional well-being. *Computers in Human Behavior,* 36, 530–541. doi: 10.1016/j.chb.2014.04.026

Couch, D., & Liamputtong, P. (2008). Online dating and mating: The use of the internet to meet sexual partners. *Qualitative Health Research,* 18(2), 268–279. https://doi.org/10.1177/1049732307312832

Crespo, E., & Freire, J.C. (2014). La atribución de responsabilidad: de la cognición al sujeto. *Psicologia and Sociedade,* 26(2), 271–279.

Darics, E., & Gatti, M.C. (2019). Talking a team into being in online workplace collaborations: The discourse of virtual work. *Discourse Studies,* 21(3), 237–257.

Davies, W. (2015). *The Happiness Industry: How the Government and Big Business Sold Us Well-Being.* London, UK: Verso Books.

Derks, D., Bos, A., & von Grumbkow, J. (2007). Emoticons and online message interpretation. *Social Science Computer Review*, 26, 379–388.

Derks, D., Fischer, A.H., & Bos, A.E.R. (2008). The role of emotion in computer-mediated communication: A review. *Computers in Human Behavior* 24(3): 766–785.

Desmet, B., & Hoste, V. (2013). Emotion detection in suicide notes. *Expert Systems with Applications*, 40(16), 6351–6358.

Dhiraj, M., & Longwell, S. (2012). Twitter and disasters. *Information, Communication and Society*, 16(6), 1–19. doi: 10.1080/1369118X.2012.696123

Dresner, E., & Herring, S.C. (2010). Functions of the nonverbal in CMC: Emoticons and illocutionary force. *Communication Theory*, 20(3), 249–268.

Dwyer, R., & Fraser, S. (2016). Addicting via hashtags: How is Twitter making addiction? *Contemporary Drug Problems*, 43(1), 79–97. doi:10.1177/0091450916637468

Eysenbach, G. (2011). Can tweets predict citations? Metrics of social impact based on Twitter and correlation with traditional metrics of scientific impact. *Journal of Medical Internet Research*, 13(4), e2012.

Gibbs, J.L., Ellison, N.B., & Lai, C.H. (2011). First comes love, then comes Google: An investigation of uncertainty reduction strategies and self-disclosure in online dating. *Communication Research*, 38(1), 70–100. https://doi.org/10.1177/0093650210377091

Giddens, A. (1991). *Modernity and Self-Identity: Self and Society in the Late Modern Age*. Stanford: Stanford University Press.

Goluboff, S. (2015). Text to sex: The impact of cell phones on hooking up and sexuality on campus. *Mobile Media & Communication*, 4(1), 102–120. https://doi.org/10.1177/2050157915603759

Greene, K., Derlega, V.J., & Mathews, A. (2006). Self-disclosure in personal relationships. In A.L. Vangelisti, & D. Perlman. *The Cambridge Handbook of Personal Relationships* (pp. 409, 427). Cambridge: Cambridge University Press.

Guedes Gondim, S.M., & Álvaro Estramiana, J.L. (2010). Naturaleza y cultura en el estudio de las emociones. *Revista Española De Sociología*, 13, 31–47.

Hadlington, L., & Scase, M.O. (2018). End-user frustrations and failures in digital technology: Exploring the role of fear of missing out, internet addiction and personality. *Heliyon*, 4(11). https://doi.org/10.1016/j.heliyon.2018.e00872

Hasan, M., Rundensteiner, E., & Agu, E. (2014). *EMOTEX: Detecting emotions in Twitter messages*. In 2014 ASE BigData/SocialCom/CyberSecurity Conference. Standford. CA.

Haythornthwaite, C. (2005). Social networks and Internet connectivity effects. *Information, Community & Society*, 8(2), 125–147.

Helles, R. (2013). Mobile communication and intermediality. *Mobile Media & Communication*, 1(1), 14–19. doi: 10.1177/2050157912459496

Henrich, J., Heine, S.J., & Norenzayan, A. (2010). The weirdest people in the world? *The Behavioral and Brain Sciences*, 33, 61–83; discussion 83–135.

Hinsch, C., & Sheldon, K. (2013). The impact of frequent social Internet consumption: Increased procrastination and lower life satisfaction. *Journal of Consumer Behaviour*, 12(6), 496–505. doi: 10.1002/cb.1453

Hobbs, M., Owen, S., & Gerber, L. (2017). Liquid love? Dating apps, sex, relationships and the digital transformation of intimacy. *Journal of Sociology*, 53(2), 271–284. https://doi.org/10.1177/1440783316662718

Hobbs, W., Burke, M., Christakis, N., & Fowler, J. (2016). Online social integration is associated with reduced mortality risk. *Proceedings of the National Academy of Sciences*, 113(46), 12980–12984. https://doi.org/10.1073/pnas.1605554113

Hochschild, A. (2019). Emotions and society. *Emotions and Society*, 1(1), 9–13. https://doi.org/10.1332/263168919X1558083641180

Honneth, A. (2004). Organized self-realization: Some paradoxes of individualization. *European Journal of Social Theory*, 7(4), 463–478.

Illouz, E. (2007). *Cold Intimacies: The Making of Emotional Capitalism*. Cambridge: Polity.

Illouz, E. (2008). *Cold Intimacies. the Making of Emotional Capitalism*. New York, NY: Polity.

Illouz, E. (2012). *Why Love Hurts: A Sociological Explanation*. Cambridge: Polity.

Jacobsen, M.H. (2019). Liquid-modern emotions: exploring Zygmunt Bauman's contribution to the sociology of emotions. *Emotions and Society*, 1(1), 99–116. https://doi.org/10.1332/263168919X15580836411878

Jansen, B.J., Zhang, M., Sobel, K., & Chowdury, A. (2009). Twitter power: Tweets as electronic word of mouth. *Journal of the American Society for Information Science and Technology*, 60(11), 2169–2188.

Jeong, B., Yoon, J., & Lee, J.M. (2017). Social media mining for product planning: A product opportunity mining approach based on topic modeling and sentiment analysis. *International Journal of Information Management*, 48, 280–290. doi: 10.1016/j.ijinfomgt.2017.09.009

Jokinen, J.P.P., 2015. Emotional user experience: traits, events, and states. *International Journal of Human-Computer Studies*, 76, 67–77. https://doi.org/10.1016/j.ijhcs.2014.12.006

Joshi, A., Tripathi, V., Soni, R., Bhattacharyya, P., & Carman, M.J. (2016, March). Emogram: an open-source time sequence-based emotion tracker and its innovative applications. In *Workshops at the thirtieth AAAI conference on artificial intelligence*.

Jurgenson, N. (2012). When atoms meet bits: Social media, the mobile web and augmented revolution. *Future Internet*, 4(1), 83–91. https://doi.org/10.3390/fi4010083

Kafeza, E., Kanavos, A., Makris, C., & Vikatos, P. (2014). T-pice: twitter personality based influential communities extraction system. In *2014 IEEE International Congress on Big Data* (pp. 212–219). Anchorage, AK.

Kao, E.C.C., Liu, C.C., Yang, T.H., Hsieh, C.T., & Soo, V.W. (2009, April). Towards text-based emotion detection a survey and possible improvements. In *2009 International Conference on Information Management and Engineering* (pp. 70–74). IEEE.

Karapanos, E., Teixeira, P., & Gouveia, R. (2016). Need fulfillment and experiences on social media: a case on Facebook and WhatsApp. *Computers in Human Behavior*, 55(1), 888–897. doi:10.1016/j.chb.2015.10.015

Kavanagh, B. (2010). A cross-cultural analysis of Japanese and English non-verbal online communication: The use of emoticons in weblogs. *Intercultural Communication Studies*, 19(3), 65–80.

Kivran-Swaine, F., & Naaman, M. (2011, November/December). *Network properties and social sharing of emotions in social awareness streams*. In Paper presented at the ACM 2011 Conference on Computer-Supported Cooperative Work (pp. 379–382). Hangzhou, China.

Kramer, A.D.I., Guillory, J.E., & Hancock, J.T. (2014). Experimental evidence of massive-scale emotional contagion through social networks. *Proceedings of the National Academy of Sciences*, 111(24), 8788–8790. doi: 10.1073/pnas.1320040111

Ku, Y.C., Chu, T.H., & Tseng, C.H. (2013). Gratifications for using CMC technologies: A comparison among SNS, IM, and e-mail. *Computers in Human Behavior*, 29, 226–234. doi: 10.1016/j.chb.2012.08.009

Langens, T. (2005). Written emotional expression and emotional well-being: The moderating role of fear of rejection. *Personality and Social Psychology Bulletin*, 31(6), 818–830. doi: 10.1177/0146167204271556

Lapinski, M.K., & Rimal, R.N. (2005). An explication of social norms. *Communication Theory*, 15(2), 127–147. https://doi.org/10.1111/j.1468-2885.2005.tb00329.x

Layard, R. (2005). *Happiness: Lessons from a New Science*. London, UK: Allen.
Leary, M.R., & Kowalski, R.M. (1990). Impression management: A literature review and two-component model. *Psychological Bulletin*, 107(1), 34.
Lin, H., Tov, W., & Qiu, L. (2014). Emotional disclosure on social networking sites: the role of network structure and psychological needs. *Computers in Human Behavior*, 41(1), 342–350. doi: 10.1016/j.chb.2014.09.045
Lup, K., Trub, L., & Rosenthal, L. (2015). Instagram #Instasad?: Exploring associations among Instagram use, depressive symptoms, negative social comparison, and strangers followed. *Cyberpsychology, Behavior, and Social Networking*, 18(5), 247–252. doi: 10.1089/cyber.2014.0560
Markman, K.M., & Oshima, S. (2007). Pragmatic play? Some possible functions of English emoticons and Japanese kaomoji in computer-mediated discourse. In *Association of Internet Researchers Annual Conference* (Vol. 8).
Martínez-Guzmán, A., & Lara, A. (2019). Affective modulation in positive psychology's regime of happiness. *Theory & Psychology*, 29(3), 336–357.
Martínez, E., Martín, M.T., Ureña, A., & Montejo, A. (2012). Sentiment analysis in Twitter. *Natural Language Engineering*. 20(1), 1–28. doi: 10.1017/S1351324912000332
Marwick, A., & Boyd, D. (2011). I tweet honestly, I tweet passionately: Twitter users, context collapse, and the imagined audience. *New Media & Society*, 13(1), 114–133. doi: 10.1177/1461444810365313
McEwan, B. (2013). Sharing, caring, and surveilling: An actor–partner interdependence model examination of Facebook relational maintenance strategies. *Cyberpsychology, Behavior, and Social Networking*, 16, 863–869. doi: 10.1089/cyber.2012.0717
McLuhan, M. (1964). The medium is the message. In *Understanding Media: The Extensions of Man* (pp. 23–35). New York: Signet.
Meredith, J., & Stokoe, E. (2014). Repair: Comparing Facebook 'chat' with spoken interaction. *Discourse & Communication*, 8(2), 181–207. https://doi.org/10.1177/1750481313510815
Mohammad, S.M., & Kiritchenko, S. (2015). Using hashtags to capture fine emotion categories from tweets. *Computational Intelligence*, 31(2), 301–326.
Nabi, R.L., Prestin, A., & So, J. (2013). Facebook friends with (health) benefits? Exploring social network site use and perceptions of social support, stress, and well-being. *Cyberpsychology, Behavior, and Social Networking*, 16, 721–727. doi: 10.1089/cyber.2012.0521
Newett, L., Churchill, B., & Robards, B. (2018). Forming connections in the digital era: Tinder, a new tool in young Australian intimate life. *Journal of Sociology*, 54(3), 346–361. https://doi.org/10.1177/1440783317728584
Paasonen, S. (2015). As networks fail: Affect, technology, and the notion of the user. *Television & New Media* 16(8), 701–716. https://doi.org/10.1177/1527476414552906
Park, N., Kee, K.F., & Valenzuela, S. (2009). Being immersed in social networking environment: Facebook groups, uses and gratifications, and social outcomes. *Cyberpsychology and Behavior*, 12, 729–733. doi: 10.1089/cpb.2009.0003
Parker, I. (2007). *Revolution in Psychology: Alienation to Emancipation*. London: Pluto Press.
Paul, M., & Dredze, M. (2011). You are what you tweet: Analyzing Twitter for public health. In *Proceedings of the International AAAI Conference on Web and Social Media* (Vol. 5, No. 1, pp. 265–272).
Pennebaker, J., Mehl, M., & Niederhoffer, K. (2003). Psychological aspects of natural language use: Our words, our selves. *Annual Review of Psychology*, 54(1), 547–577. doi: 10.1146/annurev.psych.54.101601.145041
Postmes, T., Spears, R., & Lea, M. (2000). The formation of group norms in computer-mediated communication. *Human Communication Research*, 26(3), 341–371. doi: 10.1111/j.1468-2958.2000.tb00761.x

Radcliffe, A., Lumley, M., Kendall, J., Stevenson, J.K., & Beltran, J. (2010). Written emotional disclosure: Testing whether social disclosure matters. *Journal of Social and Clinical Psychology*, 26(3), 362–384. doi: 10.1521/jscp.2007.26.3.362

Rainie, L., & Wellman, B. (2012). *Networked: The New Social Operating System*. Cambridge, MA: MIT Press. https://doi.org/10.7551/mitpress/8358.001.0001

Rathore, A.K., & Ilavarasan, P.V. (2018). Social media and business practices. In *Encyclopedia of Information Science and Technology*, Fourth edition (pp. 7126–7139). Hershey, PA: IGI Global.

Reinecke, L., & Trepte, S. (2014). Authenticity and well-being on social network sites: a two-wave longitudinal study on the effects of online authenticity and the positivity bias in SNS communication. *Computers in Human Behavior*, 30(1), 95–102. doi: 10.1016/j.chb.2013.07.030

Rentschler, C. (2015). # Safetytipsforladies: Feminist Twitter takedowns of victim blaming. *Feminist Media Studies*, 15(2), 353–356. doi: 10.1080/14680777.2015.1008749

Rose, A.J. (2002). Co-rumination in the friendships of girls and boys. *Child Development*, 73(6), 1830–1843. doi: 10.1111/1467–8624.00509

Sailunaz, K., & Alhajj, R. (2019). Emotion and sentiment analysis from Twitter text. *Journal of Computational Science*, 36, 101003.

Sampietro, A. (2016). *Emoticonos y emojis: Análisis de su historia, difusión y uso en la comunicación digital actual* (Tesis doctoral). Universitat de València.

Sampietro, A. (2019). Emoji and rapport management in Spanish WhatsApp chats. *Journal of Pragmatics*, 143, 109–120. https://doi.org/10.1016/j.pragma.2019.02.009

Santos Ortega, A., Serrano-Pascual, A., Borges, E. (2021). El dispositivo emprendedor: Interpelación ética y producción de nuevos sujetos del trabajo. *Revista Española de Sociología*, 30(3), a62 https://doi.org/10.22325/fes/res.2021.62

Seligman, M. (2012). *Flourishing: A Visionary New Understanding of Happiness and Wellbeing*. New York, NY: Free Press.

Sheldon, P., & Bryant, K. (2016) Instagram: motives for its use and relationship to narcissism and contextual age. *Computers in Human Behavior*, 58(1), 89–97. doi: 10.1016/j.chb.2015.12.059

Shirdastian, H., Laroche, M., & Richard, M.O. (2017). Using big data analytics to study brand authenticity sentiments: The case of Starbucks on Twitter. *International Journal of Information Management*: https://doi.org/10.1016/j.ijinfomgt.2017.09.007

Slater, D. (2013). *Love in the Time of Algorithms: What Technology Does to Meeting and Mating*. New York: Penguin Group.

Skovholt, K., Grønning, A., & Kankaanranta, A. (2014). The communicative functions of emoticons in workplace e-mails::-). *Journal of Computer-Mediated Communication*, 19(4), 780–797. https://doi.org/10.1111/jcc4.12063

Sohn, D. (2014). Coping with information in social media: The effects of network structure and knowledge on perception of information value. *Computers in Human Behavior*, 32, 145–151. doi: 10.1016/j.chb.2013.12.006

Sprecher, S. (2009). Relationship initiation and formation on the Internet. *Marriage & Family Review*, 45(6–8), 761–782. https://doi.org/10.1080/01494920903224350

Statista. (2019). *Twitter: Number of monthly active users 2010–2019*. Recuperado en Abril, 2020, from www.statista.com/statistics/282087/number-of-monthly-active- twitter-users/

Szto, C., & Gray, S. (2015). Forgive me father for I have thinned: Surveilling the bio-citizen through Twitter. *Qualitative Research in Sport, Exercise and Health*, 7, 321–337. doi: 10.1080/2159676X.2014.938245

Taddicken, M. (2014). The 'privacy paradox' in the social web: the impact of privacy concerns, individual characteristics, and the perceived social relevance on different forms of self-disclosure. *Journal of Computer-Mediated Communication*, 19(2), 248–273. doi: 10.1111/jcc4.12052

Taquet, M., Quoidbach, J., de Montjoye, Y., Desseilles, M., & Gross, J. (2016). Hedonism and the choice of everyday activities. *Proceedings of the National Academy of Sciences*, 113(35), 9769–9773. https://doi.org/10.1073/pnas.1519998113

Thornton, L. (2013). 'Time of the month' on Twitter: Taboo, stereotype and bonding in a no-holds-barred public arena. *Sex Roles*, 68, 41–54. doi: 10.1177/1461444809360773.

Turner, J.H., & Stets, J.E. (2004). *The Sociology of Emotions*. Cambridge: Cambridge University Press. https://doi.org/10.1017/CBO9780511819612

Twenge, J.M. (2017). *iGen: Why Today's Super-Connected Kids Are Growing Up Less Rebellious, More Tolerant, Less Happy – and Completely Unprepared for Adulthood – and What that Means for the Rest of Us*. New York: Simon and Schuster.

Uski, S., & Lampinen, A. (2016). Social norms and self-presentation on social network sites: Profile work in action. *New Media & Society*, 18(3), 447–464.

Vanden Abeele, M., Schouten, A.P., & Antheunis, M.L. (2016). Personal, editable, and always accessible: An affordance approach to the relationship between adolescents' mobile messaging behavior and their friendship quality. *Journal of Social and Personal Relationships*, 34(6), 875–893. doi: 10.1177/0265407516660636

Vandergriff, I. (2013). Emotive communication online: a contextual analysis of computer-mediated communication (CMC) cues. *Journal Pragmatics*, 51, 1–12. https://doi.org/10.1016/j.pragma.2013.02.008

Waterloo, S., Baumgartner, S., Peter, J., & Valkenburg, P. (2017). Norms of online expressions of emotion: Comparing Facebook, Twitter, Instagram, and WhatsApp. *New Media & Society*, 20(5), 1813–1831. doi: 10.1177/1461444817707349

Weller, K., Bruns, A., Burgess, J., Mahrt, M., & Puschmann, C. (2014). Twitter and society: An introduction. *Twitter and Society [Digital Formations, Volume 89]*, xxix–xxxviii.

Wilson, A. (1993). A pragmatic device in electronic communication. *Journal Pragmatics*, 19(4), 389–398. https://doi.org/10.1016/0378-2166(93)90098-A

Wittgenstein, L. (1958). *Philosophical Investigations*. Oxford: Basil Blackwell.

Yus, F. (2014). Not all emoticons are created equal. *Linguagem em (Dis)curso*, 14(3), 511–529. https://doi.org/10.1590/1982-4017-140304-0414

Zickuhr, K. (2013). *Who's Not Online and Why*. Pew Research Center. Internet & Technology.

4
BETWEEN THE COLLECTIVITY OF EMOTIONS AND EMOTIONAL CONTAGION

The social turn

In this chapter, we examine the collectivity and the sharing of emotions in society, a concept that has worried psychologists and social scientists in recent years. We present here different perspectives and settings where these emotions can be studied, from social movements to artistic companies. We present different research about the collectivity nature of emotions and emotional contagion in different groups that have been analyzed, and the communicative and synchronization dynamics that underlie subjective processes. We conclude this chapter with a few examples from the pandemic time that we have lived in recent years. A diffuse, dispersed, and liquid shared emotion, in this case the fear, is perfect to understand the emotional contagion in society. Following this direction, we develop the social turn of the emotions to study the interpersonal cognitive processes and collective emotions, decisions, and so on.

4.1 Collectivities and movements

In recent years, there has been an increase in literature on the social turn of emotions from different perspectives and traditions. For example, collective emotions are part of a research area that combines studies from philosophy, anthropology, sociology, and psychology. Collective emotions are manifestations of widely shared feelings (Sullivan, 2015). This type of emotions are different from individual emotions because they are the result of acting and feeling together as a group. One of the major challenges faced by any social group when exposed to a collective threat is the development of a coordinated, cooperative response to it (Cosmides & Tooby, 2013). Collective rituals have most likely been part of group functioning since the dawn of humanity and are considered central to coordinated and cooperative performance in large social groups (Durkheim, 1915; Rossano, 2012; Watson-Jones & Legare, 2016). The key idea is that 'after an emotional event, individuals will initiate

DOI: 10.4324/9781003247999-5

interpersonal behaviours in which discussing this event and their reactions to it is central' (Rimé et al., 1991: 436). Some researchers define collective emotions as group-based emotions being spread between various subjects (Goldenberg et al., 2014; von Scheve & Ismer, 2013). A collective emotion is a multifaceted emotional reaction whose factors are spread among various individuals and is a complex procedure of socially distributed components based on dynamical social interaction (Thonhauser, 2022). Collective emotions are also experienced with first-person plural consciousness in a We-mode (Schmid, 2014).

The collective emotion is the emotion of a collective, but this definition is vague and ambiguous and often used in a general way in psychology and social science. Emotions in collectives are structurally complex and are socially distributed. These collective emotions incorporate and interact with emotions that individuals feel on behalf of their group as a result of identification with others (Ray, Mackie & Smith, 2014). Research on collective emotions has highlighted specific instances of group pride, shame, guilt, anger, and fear, to understand the collective behaviour of people in social movements and community activities, for example (Sullivan, 2015). Collective rituals are a powerful source of positive emotions towards other members of the group or community, which in turn encourages adherence to prosocial norms and the suspension of immediate self-interest (Rossano, 2012). Emotional synchrony experienced by individuals during collective events has been shown to mediate between participation in rituals and greater social cohesion and integration, as well as higher endorsement of social beliefs and values (Páez et al., 2015).

For Thonhauser (2022), when collective emotions emerge they have different structural features. First, a collective perspective which leads to a joint focus of the emotion; later, a collective evaluation of the eliciting episode leading to the similar emotional responses among members, followed by an awareness of intimacy, that sense that collective emotions derive with first-person plural consciousness (We-mode) of the emotion.

Thanks to this introduction, we can now observe with several examples from our research, how emotions are related to collectives and society. We have been able to observe how emotions have acquired a leading role in today's society to explain many of the aspects that concern human beings. An emblematic example of how collective emotions have impacted society can be found in the emerging social movements in recent years, like the Occupy movement in 2011 and the movement against climate change, Fridays For Future, in 2019. Both have been born and have expanded in cities on different continents in the last decade. Participants in these movements have been characterized by an emotional attachment based on trust in the collective and in their joint action. We can identify different emotions in these social movements because activists and participants have lived and felt it, provoking the need to share similar experiences and make their emotions socially visible, for example a group that establishes affective bonds with those who share the same emotions protesting in a public space. This collectivity of emotions facilitates intersubjective connection and reinforces the collective identity of activists and participants who at a certain moment occupy a public space like a place or a street as a form of protest (Belli & Díez, 2015). People may group together on the basis of positive emotions or negative emotions (Sullivan, 2015). Successful interaction rituals transform the previous emotion and 'create new higher-order social emotions out of more primitive emotions' (Collins, 2014: 300).

But for Sullivan (2015), this neo-Durkheimian framework fails to consider collective mixed emotions. For example, the solidarity that is felt from participating in a commemoration, may be experienced ambivalently by an individual or group. For him, it is possible for groups to display qualitatively distinct states, which are experienced either in quick succession or simultaneously towards the same object or target (Sullivan, 2015):

> A further example is the transformation in Germany that occurred during the 2006 World Cup: prior to the tournament, it had largely been taboo to wave a German flag or wear the national colours of Germany because of associations with extreme right-wing, neo-Nazi groups (Sullivan, 2009, 2014). The 'carnival' of the World Cup transformed the relation of many German citizens to their nation from one of shame, ambivalence and distancing to celebration and collective pride. Moreover, positive emotions at the time were described as an apolitical and celebratory 'party patriotism' (Sullivan, 2009), even though any national identity assumes an ideology of individual national states (Billig, 1995).
>
> *p.385*

This example helps us to understand and clarify why collective emotions cannot be considered a shared individual emotion. It is not a bottom-up dynamic, where individuals share their I-mode emotions as global We-mode emotions. And neither is there a top-down dynamic where in the collectivity of We-mode emotions each individual agrees with the same collective emotion in an I-mode. The issues are more complex. Tuomela (2013) helps us to analyze this group agency and collective intentionality to give an overview from a critical social and psychological perspective. An important insight from the social ontology perspective on collective emotions (Salmela, 2012) is the distinction between ideal forms of We-mode and I-mode. We-mode feeling as a group is central to understanding collective phenomena because 'the social world cannot be adequately explained and rationally understood without postulating groups as intentional agents' (Tuomela, 2013: 2). The We-mode approach occupies the middle ground between reduction of group action to the intentional behaviour of individuals. Tuomela's framework is an important critical resource for a social science and psychology of collective emotion, because it highlights the limitations of current trends in theorizing and research (Sullivan, 2015).

Also artistic movements have been observed to analyze the communicative and synchronization dynamics that underlie subjective processes from an I-mode to a We-mode to express emotions (Muntanyola-Saura & Belli, 2014; 2016). This change in the unit of analysis serves to better explain the emotional elements that affect the processes of artistic work, and to avoid errors and unforeseen events between artists who work as a team and not as individuals. A greater understanding of the collective emotions of a team would greatly limit errors and accidents when thinking about the creative and professional process of the entire activity. In a study in a contemporary dance company (Muntanyola-Saura & Belli, 2014; 2016), based on interviews with the dancers, choreographers, and musicians, collective emotions are empirically observable thanks to the narratives produced by participants explaining their profession routine in the company. Thanks to the delimitation of subjective processes (I-mode), crucial in the study of emotions, we can understand how some dynamics are manifested, through rejection and identification in the group (We-mode). The two processes have to do with the social and discursive relationship of the members of the dance company, and the rejection (or identification) of the image and the traits assigned to the group from other groups (the construction of a negative image of 'them', for example). It will also be possible to observe, thanks to linguistic differentiation, the rejection (or identification) of the rules and routines of the others. It is an emotional phase in which the dancer narrates the music and the movement, relating to the steps her body takes when listening to it. The music and the dancer build an emotional relationship from an I-mode. The image of the body is the representation that the dancer makes of her body; the way she appears to her through the social and cultural context. But we understand dance not only as body movement accompanied by music, but also as discursive productions through collectivity of emotions. All the emotions that can be transmitted, heard, and felt, thanks to music affecting the body, and shared in a We-mode, like a dance step or a movement between dancers. This music accompanies the movement and catalyzes certain emotions from I-mode to We-mode, like the continuous movement of our leg as an escape route to synchronize our movement with the others.

Research confirms that the body performs through music, and it is possible to relate music, bodies, and emotions. The dancer's bodily gesture expresses an emotion that is not 'behind the gesture', but rather identifies with it. If we observe someone listening to music with headphones on, we see how they move in different rhythms, and we can almost guess what kind of music they are listening to. Depending on the intensity of the movement, we can interpret that they are listening to slow music if their body moves slowly, or on the contrary, when we see this person jump and move their arms up, we intuit that they are listening to some energetic and moving melody. The body embodies this music, and music provokes emotions. We can affirm that the physical representation of emotions with music makes dance performance possible. Musicians and dancers trained in emotional performance are much more skilled in regulating emotions, both internally and externally (Damasio, 1999: 50). This difference shows that the activity of listening to music is also learned, and that it is socially localized. This complex experience is, above all, collective: in Aaron Fox's (2004) study of the identity that country music can give to a southern population, there is talk of the existence of a musical community. A community made up of 'abstract domains of memory, place, models of the self, emotions and feeling, and the concrete things of everyday life, such as sociability, sensuality, work and play' (Fox, 2004: 34). Fox goes a step further and includes the weight of collective emotions that unite those who share the same musical experience.

4.2 Recognition, imitation, and performance

The complexity of the study of emotions comes from taking into account one's own personal experience as a rich and, at times, chaotic source of data (Belli & Broncano, 2017). We agree with Rom Harré (2000) that language is the main instrument through which such emotional constructions and experiences arise. The concept of performance and emotions that we have introduced in chapter one helps us to present the psychosociological context in which we observe the management of affects within the framework of interdependence. This section will seek answers to our question aimed at assessing the interdependence framework in the context of the COVID-19 pandemic. In this way, we ask ourselves what the role of emotional contagion is in the way people behave during the current pandemic and how emotions are spread from person to person.

For van Kleef & Cote (2022), emotional contagion is a set of processes by which observers come to feel the same emotions that others express. Emotional expressions provide information about the expresser's experiences and appraisals of situations (Manstead & Fischer, 2001, Scherer & Grandjean, 2008). This process involves the use of emotion knowledge to extract information from others' emotional expressions (van Kleef & Cote, 2022). In Lundqvist & Dimberg's study (1995), participants exposed to pictures showing emotional expressions reported experiencing similar feelings themselves. Studies revealed that emotional states spread in teams of professionals (Totterdell et al., 1998) and players (Totterdell, 2000).

Von Scheve and Ismer (2013) argue for the importance of joint attention as the basis upon which collective emotions can be built, developmentally and culturally, and a focus on 'bottom-up' mechanisms – particularly mimicry of facial expressions or mutual awareness between individuals – as the central means by which processes of emotional contagion occur in crowd and group situations. Emotional contagion is the experience of one's own mood changing and being intensified by the emotions of other people (Sullivan, 2015). Margaret Wetherell (2012) emphasizes the discursive repertoires available to produce and reproduce the conditions and practices that afford collective emotions. Wetherell (2012) gives a rich overview of alternative possibilities of the circulation of emotions that can occur in parliamentary committees or in football where the affective-discursive genres, and personal and social histories channel communal emotions.

We have observed up to this point that emotional contagion can occur at conscious levels, thanks to the processes of social comparison and discourses in which people evaluate their emotions in comparison with those of other subjects and respond with what seems appropriate according to the context (Barsade, 2002; Schachter, 1959; Sullins, 1991). But people also influence each other unintentionally and possibly even unknowingly. The sociologist Gabriel Tarde (1903) has provided a useful analytical distinction on intentional and unintentional influence. For Tarde, we may not be able to document all types of influences that affect people and show through imitation and contamination between them, but we can analyze them from their narratives and experiences. It should be clear that imitation and contamination denote constructions or fabrications (to use a common term also with Butler's approach) and repetition processes in the social world, indicating only socially learned acts by observation that are then performed. Tarde (1903) studied a general change in the mode of social reproduction of customs, that is, the epidemic and endemic horizontal transmission where society is always and only pure imitation. By 'generative imitation' Tarde meant a process that he conceptualized in terms of the combination of existing imitations, that is, the 'fruitful interference of repetitions'. On the other hand, he used the term 'imitative imitation' to define the propagation of inventions and their imitations through time and space. Tarde's basic argument was that human history could be interpreted as a 'race' of imitations, that is, of inherited trajectories of inventions through populations that differentially survive an ongoing selection process of 'counterimitation' or rejection (Marsden, 2000). Reflecting on this flow of influence and the emotional contagion in society leads one to wonder if Tarde's 'imitation' is as far away as it seems (Katz, 2006). For Katz (2006), there are good reasons to think of imitation as one of the forms that influence can take, considering the decisions with which a subject can influence (infect) some behaviour of another subject even without knowing it. The influence may have occurred even when both parties are unaware of their roles, calling this 'contagion' in the same way that epidemiologists do. For this reason, Tarde could be considered one of the pioneers in defining an interpretive framework for interdependence based on social interaction, ethnomethodology, and even actor-network theory:

> If we look at the [human] social world, the only one we know from the inside, we see the agents, the humans, much more differentiated, much more individually characterised, much richer in continuous variations, than the governmental apparatus, the system of laws and beliefs, even the dictionaries and the grammars which are maintained through their activities. An historical fact is simpler and clearer that any mental state of any of the actors [participating in it].
>
> *Tarde, 1903: 69iv, cited in Latour, 2002: 6*

We consider the pandemic as a historical event that has made visible the transfer of emotions through emotional contagion among the population, impacting the processes of interdependence. Agency, together with social influence and imitation, is exactly what Latour (2002) calls actor-network. The linking of the two ideas is essential to understand Tarde's approach, because it does not respect any border between nature and society, and because it does not stop at the border between physics, biology, and sociology, paraphrasing the reading of Latour (2002). For Tarde, all things are society and each phenomenon is a social fact, unlike Durkheim who argues that social facts should be treated as one thing (Latour, 2002). Even society is pure imitation for Tarde.

4.3 The emotional contagion

In this section, we analyze how emotional contagion has been considered at the micro level and at the macro level. At the micro level, Parkinson and Simons (2012) found that the anxiety and enthusiasm of the subjects of their study were close to significantly influence to their focal perceptions about the decisions. The importance, for example, of staying home confined is perceived differently by citizens throughout the COVID-19 pandemic. At first it was thought to be an exaggeration and then an act of responsibility. Erisen, Lodge and Taber (2014) found evidence of emotional contagion in the political evaluations of individuals. Their theory of motivated political reasoning suggests that emotions trapped in the early stages of information processing have a significant influence on the evaluation and subsequent support or rejection of them. At the macro level, the emotion that was transmitted to the policy evaluators led them to make decisions and evaluations consistent with their emotions. Throughout the pandemic, it has been observed how different transnational policies have benefited from this emotional contagion by making similar decisions when it comes to countering the virus and choosing the same strategies to put them into operation.

Throughout this pandemic, humans have followed similar patterns of emotional dependence and interdependence, from the indifference that 'the virus is something that does not affect my life' to curiosity about what is happening elsewhere and fear of the virus and its management of the crisis and death (Díez, Belli, Márquez, 2020). The progression of these emotional dependencies and interdependencies is also related to the development and establishment of responsible behaviour patterns among citizens. Individuals redefine social reality in emotional terms to face fear and uncertainty in the face of the unknown. On this occasion, they have developed social patterns of behaviour that mostly emphasize co-responsibility, solidarity and civic culture (Díez & Laraña, 2017).

Scientists have found that individuals generally respond differently to positive and negative emotional stimuli (Barsade et al., 2018). For example, negative events, such as a pandemic, generate faster and more powerful emotional, behavioural, and cognitive responses than neutral or positive events (Cacioppo, Gardner, & Berntson, 1997; Rozin & Royzman, 2001). According to the theory of motivated cognitive processing (Clark & Isen, 1982), which proposes that people can be motivated to remain in a positive affective state, there may be situations in which people instinctively focus more on positive emotions avoiding the negatives.

Social networks and digital platforms have facilitated the exchange of information and have favoured emotional contagion. As conversations and activities take place more and more virtually, academics have begun to explore whether emotional contagion can occur without physical co-location (in many cases, through just text-based interaction) (Barsade et al., 2018), where emotions can be extended virtually and without physical contact (Cheshin et al., 2011; Del Vicario et al., 2016; Ferrara & Yang, 2015; Kramer et al., 2014). Making it clear that emotional contagion is a contagion based on the textual rather than on the body.

Another social phenomenon that is probably influenced by emotional contagion is the tendency of individuals to expose themselves to information that reinforces their points of view, which contributes to an apparent 'echo chamber' within social networks and the media. (Barberá, Jost, Nagler, Tucker & Bonneau, 2015; Garrett, 2009). The emotions expressed in digital contexts, for example, are likely to lead to greater partisanship and division, as different groups are bombarded with often very different sets of emotions about the same event (Barsade et al., 2018). For this reason, emotional contagion increases the division, due to the different feelings of, for example, collective anger, joy, or relief, shared between the different subgroups (and media echo chambers) to which the subject belongs.

4.4 Fear and trust, or a new mode of existence of the subject

Bauman (2006) argues that emotions are variable and mischievous, lose momentum very quickly and tend to deviate from the initial goal with the slightest distraction. They are notoriously fickle, and they can change completely during an interaction. The crowds that form to lynch someone are unreliable; sometimes they can be moved by sorrow. Emotions are multiple and speak in different and often discordant voices. It is for this reason that Max Weber (1903) mentions reason as an element fundamental for the survival of society, because reason, unlike emotions, is one and has a single voice. And as has been said in the previous section, emotions are a performance, so every attempt to repeat these fabrications is destined to fail. It is a pity that Zygmunt Bauman did not experience this pandemic, because his conception and definition of liquid fear (2006) could be adapted to current contexts. The diffuse, dispersed, unclear fear that Bauman speaks, is the fear that we have lived during the pandemic time. It is a fear that floats free, without ties, without anchors, without a home to use the sociologist's words. Fear is also the name we give to our ignorance regarding the threat and what needs to be done to stop it. The modern liquid world that Bauman (2006) presents to us is one of which a single certainty is admitted, which involves a daily trial of disappearance and erasure. It is an artefact that aims to suppress the horror of danger, but the virus has destroyed this almost perfect device. If liquid life, according to the Polish sociologist, flowed slowly from one challenge to another, between the millennium bug and mad cow disease, it has finally encountered a real and powerful enemy.

According to the survey on Mental Health of Spaniards carried out by the Sociological Research Center (2021), 23.4% of Spaniards acknowledged that they have been afraid of dying due to COVID-19. This fear increases (68.6%) when it is considered that it is a loved one who can die in this situation. It has also been observed that fear is greater when a subject is more concerned with infecting others than with being infected.

Fear moves freely, without ties, without anchors, and without a localization. Fear is also the name we give to our ignorance regarding the threat and what it needs to be done to stop it. People are infected by virus and fear, a viral logic of how emotions may spread across populations and between people. A recently proposed model of uncertainty distress poses the 'unknownness', which characterizes the experience of COVID-19 losses (Freeston, Tiplady, Mawn, Bottesi, & Thwaites, 2020). COVID-19 deaths can be classified as ambiguous losses (Testoni et al., 2021) because the death occurs rapidly, unexpectedly for some, and farewell often must be made without the physical presence of the body (Bertuccio & Runion, 2020). Cipolletta, Entilli and Filisetti (2022) explored the experiences of the bereaved following the death of a loved one to COVID-19. The unpreparedness on the part of local administrations and healthcare systems to contain the infection and manage the health emergency may have further adversely impacted those who lost a significant person in their lives.

The lack of a funeral was considered significant by mourners, who longed for the hugs of family members and the opportunity to publicly experience their pain; this obstacle to the farewell is a great disappointment and professionals should base their interventions on the possibility of constructing a sense for what happened, possibly through the creation of meaningful rituals to replace the lost ones (Borghi & Menichetti, 2021) such as lighting a candle, holding a ceremony outdoor (e.g. in a private garden) or collecting songs, photos and stories linked to the departed (Burrell & Selman, 2020).

Mourners felt relieved thinking their experience was of shared grief with an extended group of other people. Socially shared grief could be a key binding factor for the ability to make sense of the loss, and it could be a good starting point for clinicians intending to foster meaning-making.

Another fundamental element in the implementation of measures that restrict freedom of movement and the trust in the actors who propose or impose such restrictions. Erving Goffman's 'civil inattention' (1979), or in other words, keeping one's distance, seems to be the only reasonable way to proceed. Human relationships are no longer areas of certainty and trust; instead, they have become a prolific source of anxiety (Bauman, 2006). For Remuzzi and Remuzzi (2020), the ability of the system to respond to changing circumstances has been under enormous pressure in this pandemic. The most effective way to contain this viral outbreak is to avoid close individual contact and social gatherings. In other words, confinement. The political decisions were to suspend activities in the workplace, replacing them with private spaces, our own homes. Telecommuting and digital activities have been key to continue developing our work activity. Physical proximity is a medical problem in a pandemic situation, but also an emotional one. Fear of other people is also the product of these political decisions. Emotional contagion, in this case, consists of avoiding any type of social context with the rest of the people around us. In this new context, social resilience appears as a new way of resisting. The behaviour of citizens was responsible, civic, and supportive, which gave meaning to their action as citizens in their daily lives and in their relationship with institutions. Actions of solidarity and responsibility to follow the rules at all times seem to be supported by the data presented by different sources (online survey CiudCovid 2020, CIS and IESA-CSIC in Díez, 2020).

Throughout this pandemic it has been possible to observe the management of trust and recognition that citizens attribute to their institutional referents and authority figures, and the cognitive and emotional processes that lead them to guide themselves, or not, due to criteria of responsibility in following standards and recommendations. In our framework of interdependence, trust is made up of various actions based on feelings of expectation, hope, rigour, sincerity, honesty, and frankness (Daukas, 2006; Williams, 2002). Fear mainly guides the communicative act of sharing information between agents.

4.5 Conclusion

We have observed that collective emotions and emotional contagion can occur at many different levels, including social comparison processes in which people evaluate their emotions in comparison with or influenced by others and respond with what seems appropriate in the setting, calling this 'contagion' in the same way that epidemiologists do it. An emblematic example of how collectivity of emotions and emotional contagion have impacted society can be found in the emerging social movements, such us the Fridays For Future movement against climate change and the Occupy movement. Participation has been characterized by an emotional attachment based on trust in the collective and in their joint action. Situations of crisis and change provoke in society a need to share experiences and make their emotions socially visible. Emotional contagion facilitates intersubjective connection and reinforces the collective identity of activists and supporters for example.

Studies into the social dynamics of collective emotion is frequently directed with the supposition of an imprecise and wide meaning of collective emotion. By difference, this chapter anticipated a description of collectivity of emotions and emotional contagion. The projected understanding of collective emotion is rather challenging, as it requires an extraordinary level of relational management and additional understanding, and analyzing the context where emotions emerge. But this is what we discover in several areas of social life like artistic performances, political parties, family life, or the workplace. Moreover, the chapter proposes that collectivity of emotions and emotional contagion remain evidently distinguished from group-based emotions and joint emotions. This chapter provided a set of theoretical differences and examples that can guide future studies on the multifaceted instruments underlying different forms of collective emotion.

References

Barberá, P., Jost, J.T., Nagler, J., Tucker, J.A., & Bonneau, R. (2015). Tweeting from left to right: Is online political communication more than an echo chamber? *Psychological Science*, 26(10), 1531–1542.

Barsade, S.G. (2002). The ripple effect: emotional contagion and its influence on group behavior. *Administrative Science Quarterly*, 47, 644–75.

Barsade, S.G., Coutifaris, C.G. & Pillemer, J. (2018). Emotional contagion in organizational life. *Research in Organizational Behavior*, 38, 137–151.

Bauman, Z. (2006). *Liquid fear*. Cambridge: Polity Press.

Belli, S., & Broncano, F. (2017). Trust as a meta-emotion. *Metaphilosophy*, 48(4), 430–448. https://doi.org/10.1111/meta.12255

Belli, S., & Díez, R. (2015). Una aproximación al papel de las emociones en la nueva ola de indignación global: La ocupación de espacios físicos y no-físicos. *Sistema: Revista de ciencias sociales*, 239, 83–98.

Bertuccio, R.F., & Runion, M.C. (2020). Considering grief in mental health outcomes of COVID-19. *Psychological Trauma: Theory, Research, Practice, and Policy*, 12, S87–S89. https://doi.org/10.1037/tra0000723

Billig, M. (1995). *Banal Nationalism*. London: Sage.

Borghi, L., & Menichetti, J. (2021). Strategies to cope with the COVID-related deaths among family members. *Frontiers in Psychiatry*, 12, 127. https://doi.org/10.3389/fpsyt.2021.622850

Burrell, A., & Selman, L.E. (2020). How do funeral practices impact bereaved relatives' mental health, grief and bereavement? A mixed methods review with implications for COVID-19. *OMEGA – Journal of Death and Dying*, 003022282094129. https://doi.org/10.1177/0030222820941296

Cacioppo, J.T., Gardner, W.L., & Berntson, G.G. (1997). Beyond bipolar conceptualizations and measures: The case of attitudes and evaluative space. *Personality and Social Psychology Review*, 1(1), 3–25.

Cheshin, A., Rafaeli, A., Bos, N. 2011. Anger and happiness in virtual teams: emotional influences of text and behavior on others' affect in the absence of non-verbal cues. *Organ. Behav. Hum. Decis. Process.*, 116, 2–16.

Cipolletta, S., Entilli, L., & Filisetti, S. (2022). Uncertainty, shock and anger: Recent loss experiences of first-wave COVID-19 pandemic in Italy. *Journal of Community & Applied Social Psychology*. Doi: 10.1002/casp.2604.

Clark, M.S., & Isen, A.M. (1982). Towards understanding the relationship between feeling states and social behavior. In A.H. Hastorf, & A.M. Isen (eds.), *Cognitive Social Psychology* (pp. 73–108). New York: Elsevier-North Holland.

Collins, R. (2014). Interaction ritual chains and collective effervescence. In C. von Scheve & M. Salmela (eds.), *Collective Emotions: Perspectives from Psychology, Philosophy, and Sociology* (pp. 299–311). Oxford: Oxford University Press.

Cosmides, L., & Tooby, J. (2013). Evolutionary psychology: New perspectives on cognition and motivation. *Annual Review of Psychology*, 64, 201–229. https://doi.org/10.1146/annurev.psych.121208.131628

Damasio, A. (1999). *The Feeling of What Happens: Body and Emotion in the Making of Consciousness*. New York: Harcourt Brace.

Daukas, N. (2006). Epistemic trust and social location. *Episteme: A Journal of Social Epistemology*, 3(1), 109–24.

Del Vicario, M., Bessi, A., Zollo, F., Petroni, F., Scala, A., Caldarelli, G., Stanley, E., & Quattrociocchi, W. (2016). The spreading of misinformation online. *Proceedings of the National Academy of Sciences*, 113(3), 554–559.

Díez, R. (2020). Ciudadanía y COVID-19: Entre el Leviatán y la cultura cívica en tiempo de pandemia. *Anuario de Movimientos Sociales – Betiko*, 1–26.

Díez, R. Belli, S., & Márquez, I. (2020). La COVID-19, pantallas y reflexividad social: Cómo el brote de un patógeno está afectando nuestra cotidianidad. *RES. Revista Española de Sociología*, 29(3), 759–768.

Díez García, R., & Laraña, E. (2017). *Democracia, dignidad y movimientos sociales: el surgimiento de la cultura cívica y la irrupción de los 'indignados' en la vida pública* (Vol. 308). Madrid: CIS-Centro de Investigaciones Sociológicas.

Durkheim, E. (1915). *The elementary forms of religious life*. New York: The Free Press.

Erisen, C., Lodge, M., & Taber, C.S. (2014). Affective contagion in effortful political thinking. *Political Psychology*, 35(2), 187–206.

Ferrara, E., & Yang, Z. (2015). Measuring emotional contagion in social media. *PLoS One*, 10(11), 1–14. e0142390.

Fox, A. (2004). *Real Country: Music, Language, Emotion and Sociability in Texas Working-Class Culture*. Durham: Duke University Press.

Freeston, M., Tiplady, A., Mawn, L., Bottesi, G., & Thwaites, S. (2020). Towards a model of uncertainty distress in the context of coronavirus (COVID-19). *The Cognitive Behaviour Therapist*, 13, e31. https://doi.org/10.1017/S1754470X2000029X

Garrett, R.K. (2009). Echo chambers online? Politically motivated selective exposure among Internet news users. *Journal of Computer-Mediated Communication*, 14(2), 265–285.

Goffman, E. (1979). Footing. *Semiotica*, 25(1–2), 1–30.

Goldenberg, A., Saguy, T., & Halperin, E. (2014). How group-based emotions are shaped by collective emotions: Evidence for emotional trans- fer and emotional burden. *Journal of Personality and Social Psychology*, 107(4), 581–596. https://doi.org/10.1037/a0037462

Harré, R. (2000). Social construction and consciousness. In ed. M. Velmans, *Investigating Phenomenal Consciousness* (pp. 233–253). Amsterdam: John Benjamin.

Katz, I. (2006) Rediscovering Gabriel Tarde. *Political Communication*, 23(3), 263–270.

Kramer, A.D., Guillory, J.E., & Hancock, J.T. (2014). Experimental evidence of massive-scale emotional contagion through social networks. *Proceedings of the National Academy of Sciences*, 111(24), 8788–8790.

Latour, B. (2002). Gabriel Tarde and the end of the social. In ed. P. Joyce, *The Social in Question: New Bearings in History and the Social Sciences* (pp. 117–132). London: Routledge.

Lundquist L-O, Dimberg U. 1995. Facial expressions are contagious. *Journal of Psychophysiology*, 9, 203–211.

Manstead, A.S.R., & Fischer, A.H. (2001). Social appraisal: the social world as object of and influence on appraisal processes. In ed. K.R. Scherer, A. Schorr, & T. Johnstone, *Appraisal Processes in Emotion: Theory, Research, Application* (pp. 221–32). New York: Oxford University Press.

Marsden, P. (2000). Forefathers of memetics: Gabriel Tarde and the laws of imitation. In ed. R. Finkelstein, *A memetic compendium* (pp. 1176–1180). College Park, MD: University of Maryland.

Muntanyola-Saura, D., & Belli, S. (2014). Emociones y música en movimiento. Discursos cruzados en una compañía de danza. *Trans* 18, 1–27.

Muntanyola, D., & Belli, S. (2016). The narrative value of dance communication: Habitus, musicality and emotion. *Revista de Antropologia Social*, 25(1), 133–151.

Páez, D., Rimé, B., Basabe, N., Wlodarczyk, A., & Zumeta, L. (2015). Psychosocial effects of perceived emotional synchrony in collective gatherings. *Journal of Personality and Social Psychology*, 108(5), 711.

Parkinson, B., & Simons, G. (2012). Affecting others: Social appraisal and emotion contagion in everyday decision making. *Personality and Social Psychology Bulletin*, 35(8), 1071–1084.

Ray, D.G., Mackie, D.M., & Smith, E.R. (2014). Intergroup emotion: self-categorization, emotion, and the regulation of intergroup conflict. In C. von Scheve & M. Salmela (eds.), *Collective Emotions: Perspectives from Psychology, Philosophy, and Sociology* (pp. 235–250). Oxford: Oxford University Press.

Remuzzi, A., & Remuzzi, G. (2020). COVID-19 and Italy: what next? *The Lancet.* doi: 10.1016/S0140-6736(20)30627-9

Rimé, B., Mesquita, B., Philippot, P., & Boca, S. (1991). Beyond the emotional event: Six studies on the social sharing of emotion. *Cognition and Emotion*, 5, 435–465.

Rossano, M.J. (2012). The essential role of ritual in the transmission and reinforcement of social norms. *Psychological Bulletin*, 138(3), 529–549. https://doi.org/10.1037/a0027038

Rozin, P., & Royzman, E.B. (2001). Negativity bias, negativity dominance, and contagion. *Personality and Social Psychology Review*, 5(4), 296–320.

Salmela, M. (2012). Shared emotions. *Philosophical Explorations*, 15(1), 33–46. https://doi.org/10.1080/13869795.2012.647355

Schachter, S. (1959). *The Psychology of Affiliation*. Stanford, CA: Stanford University Press.

Scherer, K., & Grandjean, D. (2008). Facial expressions allow inference of both emotions and their components. *Cognition & Emotion*, 22, 789–801.

Schmid, H.B. (2014). The feeling of being a group: corporate emotions and collective consciousness. In C. von Scheve & M. Salmela (eds.), *Collective Emotions: Perspectives from Psychology, Philosophy, and Sociology* (pp. 3–16). Oxford: Oxford University Press.

Sullins, E. (1991). Emotional contagion revisited: Effects of social comparison and expressive style on mood convergence. *Personality and Social Psychology*, 17(2), 166–174.

Sullivan, G.B. (2009). Germany during the 2006 World Cup: The role of television in creating a national narrative of pride and 'party patriotism'. In E. Castelló, A. Dhoest & H. O'Donnell (eds.), *The Nation on Screen: Discourses of the National in Global Television* (pp. 235–252). Cambridge: Cambridge Scholars Press.

Sullivan, G.B. (2014). Collective emotions, German national pride and the 2006 World Cup. In G.B. Sullivan (ed.), *Understanding Collective Pride and Group Identity: New Directions in Emotion Theory, Research and Practice* (pp. 124–136). London: Routledge.

Sullivan, G.B. (2015). Collective emotions. *Social and Personality Psychology Compass*, 9(8), 383–393.

Tarde, G. (1903). *The Laws of Imitation*. New York: H. Holt.

Testoni, I., Azzola, C., Tribbia, N., Biancalani, G., Iacona, E., Orkibi, H., & Azoulay, B. (2021). The COVID-19 disappeared: From traumatic to ambiguous loss and the role of the internet for the bereaved in Italy. *Frontiers in Psychiatry*, 12, 564. https://doi.org/10.3389/fpsyt.2021.620583

Thonhauser, G. (2022). Towards a taxonomy of collective emotions. *Emotion Review*, 17540739211072469.

Totterdell, P. (2000). Catching moods and hitting runs: Mood linkage and subjective performance in professional sport teams. *Journal of Applied Psychology*, 85, 848–859.

Totterdell, P., Kellett, S., Teuchmann, K., Briner, B. (1998). Evidence of mood linkage in work groups. *Journal of Personality Social Psychology*, 74, 1504–1515.

Tuomela, R. (2013). *Social Ontology: Collective Intentionality and Group Agents*. Oxford: Oxford University Press.

van Kleef, G.A., & Côté, S. (2022). The social effects of emotions. *Annual Review of Psychology*, 73, 629–658.

von Scheve, C., & Ismer, S. (2013). Towards a theory of collective emotions. *Emotion Review*, 5(4), 1–8. https://doi.org/10.1177/1754073913484170

Watson-Jones, R.E., & Legare, C.H. (2016). The social functions of group rituals. *Current Directions in Psychological Science*, 25(1), 42–46. https://doi.org/10.1177/0963721415618486

Weber, M. (1903 (2003)). *La Ética protestante y el espíritu del capitalismo*. Buenos Aires: Fondo de Cultura Economica.

Wetherell, M. (2012). *Affect and Emotion: A New Social Science Understanding*. London: Sage.

Williams, P. 2002. The Competent Boundary Spanner. *Public Administration*, 80(1), 103–24.

5
WORKING WITH EMOTIONS
The management turn

In this last chapter, we conclude our exploration about emotions by observing how these work inside in professional contexts like academia. With a critical perspective, we analyze emotions that academics and researchers feel every day in their institutional spaces like laboratories and offices. We explore the emotional dimension of the strategies that researchers use to collaborate and cooperate between them. Hence, we highlight that the emotional work of researchers consists in combining different emotional strategies by activating and deactivating affection, warmth and spontaneity in their professional interactions.

In this chapter, we provide a review of the literature on scientific collaboration from a critical perspective to understand emotions, examining the discursively constructed nature of scientific collaborations and the role of emotions in organizational contexts and leadership forms. We present the result of our own analysis, investigating the contrast between the individual and the group dimension when speaking about scientific practices. We also show how these logics can be fostered from leadership positions and how this is based on dynamics that involve emotional work on the group. We conclude with a critical discussion of the work in academia, as an example of a space charged with emotions.

Before analyzing emotions in science, we want to present an example based on the text by Bruno Latour (2017) on the scientific world. Latour introduced the figure, Pierre Kernowicz. Pierre Kernowicz is no longer a young promise who was lent a corner to see if he could find something in his name, he is no longer a small craftsman who works with some technicians on high-risk issues. He runs a kind of small and medium business in the scientific market. Three or four people work for him.

For Latour (2017), the investigator is a strange hybrid; depending on the moment of his career, he is a worker, a manager, a small boss, a large capitalist, and again an artisan. He seems to defy the rules of economics – at least he prides himself on

DOI: 10.4324/9781003247999-6

it – but perhaps he rigorously follows those of capital. We have seen with what spirit Pierre refuses to be someone else's coach, and so how he becomes a boss and twice refuses to let others buy from him. The principle is very simple: only those who control the entire cycle can expect to accumulate large sums. The ideal is to also control that part of the cycle in which the money is distributed.

Pierre is not a 'big capitalist', but a boss of small and medium-sized companies. He certainly controls the entire cycle, but none of the instances that support that cycle. As a small boss, he himself still works in the corner and accumulates a part of his credibility with his own hands. He has technicians, but he doesn't like the role they play. The technician is clearly exploited like any other employee: he sells his work for a salary. Without a title, he cannot pass into the cycle of capital. After twenty years of scientific work, he will be at the same point (unless he is able to pass the thesis), even if Pierre establishes in his laboratory the scientific equivalent of profits: he always puts the names of the technicians on the articles ('makes them work better') and are paid 'like doctors'. Thus, at least in theory, part of the group's credibility belongs to his name. But in reality, of course, they can't get a grant or even a scholarship on their own.

Very different is the case of the few doctors that Pierre hired with his own funds. They work for him, although in theory they could apply for a grant and set up on their own. Unlike the technicians he values, Pierre cuts them short to build credibility on his own behalf and not theirs. If they want to be independent, they can be, but they must contribute their own money; 'if they work with my funds, they have to do what I tell them'.

The rivalry between the chief and the investigators is well known; although equal in titles, some have the money and control of the cycle and others do not, but they can become bosses depending on the circumstances. Pierre slightly underestimates his investigators who have not had the will to work alone from the beginning like him; he prefers technicians, who can never rival him.

Thanks to the figure of Pierre we can understand the context in which science and scientists move in their daily work and the wide range of emotions that he and his collaborators experiment with every day, combining leadership and research experience. Thanks to him, we can introduce how emotions matter in our work contexts.

5.1 Career and collaboration in research

Only a third of graduate students who completed a PhD continue on in the research field, and the others experience either a change in their career preference or difficulties in their career progression in academia (Ranieri et al., 2016). There is a commonly known pressure in academia known as 'publish or perish'; this stress can lead to be too much for some, however those with higher levels of self-efficacy, hope, gratitude, and optimism are known to experience less stress. The motivating factor to be successful also brings a high amount of career satisfaction. While barriers may include failure to get an article published, or a research proposal accepted, any obstacles are seen to be overcome through determination. Apart from research, academics are also able to dedicate time to teaching, mentoring, and administrative tasks. An academician must be able to do surface acting, which is a way of coping, and hide their emotions of any distressing experiences from their students and colleagues when needing to fulfil other commitments. A career in academia also requires constant awareness of current research, theories, and developments to succeed in the field and also brings on greater competence, self-reliance, courage, and professional identity. The way academics identify and describe themselves, whether as a researcher or in any goals that they may hope to accomplish in their career, also increases their productivity, motivational energy, and ability to fulfil their career goals. It takes a very dedicated and passionate person to pursue a career in academia, described it best in saying 'You've got to love what you do. You've got to have passion for it' (Cannizzo, 2017: 104).

Santos Ortega, Serrano-Pascual and Borges (2021) present us with the figure of the entrepreneurial device, the stories that the company generates about itself to legitimize itself and perpetuate its operation as a key institution. The narration, the dramatization, the glorious self-history, the success stories constitute narrative tactics put at the service of society to request the adherence of the subjects, who are promised success if they adopt the story, assuming control of communication and possible resistance or negative emotions, discordant with the history and functioning of the organization, such as complaints due to stress, burnout, work overload, or some other conflict (Santos Ortega, Serrano-Pascual & Borges, 2021).

Santos Ortega, Serrano-Pascual and Borges (2021) argue that the spread of business rhetoric is composed of and justified by the behaviour of its workers from the workplace to their lives that goes beyond the experience at work, such as their emotions. In the latter, we are witnessing the rise of emotional intelligence, which means putting emotional engineering at the service of individual optimization and worker productivity. In the same way, individuals are called to embrace positive thinking and what Mark Fisher (2016) calls magical voluntarism: 'if you want, you can …' intimated in a thousand expressions that are transmitted daily to the subjects in a supposed activator way (Rodríguez López & Borges Gómez, 2018).

In this professional context, researchers are also encouraged to collaborate between them and there is the tendency to assert and defend this without any analysis of the complexity and heterogeneity of collaborative practices. It is not surprising to find researchers unquestionably affirming the importance of scientific collaboration. Generally, researchers refer to networks between groups that combine their resources, experiences, and infrastructures. This allows more far-reaching results. The specific virtues of interdisciplinary collaboration are sometimes emphasized as a more complex dynamic in which researchers from different fields manage to articulate common objectives. However, when talking about collaboration, teamwork is emphasized with insistence. It consists of reciprocal and interdependent relationships that seek to combine specialized skills, join forces, and enrich ideation and problem-solving processes.

In this sense, the scientific-academic field has been in a profound process of transformation for decades. Management of research groups and the role played by principal investigators (PIs) has been pluralized and substantially modified in recent decades as the result of different phenomena, such as increasing internationalization, work intensification, extension of digital mediations in information management and communication, as well as new forms of work organization and evaluation-audit. Consequently, research conducted on this field suggests that teams are experiencing contradictions between the value of collaboration, as team members are interdependent, and the mandate to fulfil a successful individual trajectory. Associated with this, there are tensions between the centrality of leadership within a vertical organizational model, which leads to the achievement of scientific objectives, and the organic and more horizontal participation structure of the members.

Apart from addressing issues related to work and organizations, this chapter deals with problems related to collaboration in critical psychology. Community, cooperation practices and their articulation in an increasingly individualistic global culture also concern our analysis. As social factors mediate the ways in which individuals conceive, act, and relate to communities, is an issue that appears throughout all the text. Following Richard Sennett (2012), we defend that starting from habits, competencies and emotions displayed in specific social and organizational contexts is a privileged way to access the power and conflict relationships that our interdependent condition as social subjects entail.

Fernández Porta (2022) draws us the current society that pushes us to be productive during working hours (LinkedIn) and in free time (Decathlon, Tinder), and that ruthless self-exploitation can only cause mental illness sooner or later. According to Santos Ortega, Serrano-Pascual and Borges (2021), the practices of strategic search for prestige and self-marketing would also be aimed in the same direction: creation of networks, articulation of networks of relationships and reputation, such as social networks and professional networks like LinkedIn and many others. In the academic world, Academia.edu and Researchgate offer visibility and reputation through which digital academics (Lupton, Mewburn & Thomson, 2017) are associated, with the general recommendation that the business world has spread for two decades. Productive networks, connections, etc., are one of the preferred representations of business reasoning since before the 1990s (Boltanski & Chiapello, 2002). They constitute a signifier that condenses innovation and the new flexible management. They are manifested in numerous practices, from business networks, collaborative work, and socio-professional relationships, to minor areas of development, such as concern for matching (the meeting of interests, work, etc.), communication and offers between businessmen; fairs, meetings, congresses, etc., where standardized business communication techniques are extended, such as demos (product demonstrations, extended, above all, among technology producers) or other communicative and relational formats such as speed dating, elevator pitch, and other proposals. In the academic world we find the thesis competitions in three minutes. With the development of technologies, the applications of these networks have multiplied and have spread to many other areas beyond work (online dating to find a partner; platforms to practice sports), and have induced a kind of calculated sociability, instrumentalized and profitable.

In the world of work, other types of business management practices are aimed at capitalizing on passion, creativity, commitment, play, for productive purposes (Zafra, 2017). An alliance is induced between personal values (and sacrifice) and valued goals to respond to higher values such as creativity, freedom, personal growth, which translate into bulimic workdays. In complicity with the culture of excess and the extension of work and creative involvement, these practices, although lived as expressions of commitment and character, can act as mechanisms of self-exploitation (sacrificial ethos, Ross, 2000) in the face of vulnerabilities that become unspeakable. In turn, with gamification and gamification practices that we have seen previously, aimed at increasing motivation, creativity, and talent development, companies introduce the logic of the game and hobbies at work. Its appeal is used to achieve goals that go beyond the entertainment contained in the game itself. With the aim of improving performance and reinforcing commitment to the task, the activity is gamified – prizes, rankings, access to higher levels. To achieve these goals, workers are required to follow certain types of behaviour that are marked by the game scheme, whose rules are immovable. Gamification breaks down the boundaries between play and work, between life and work.

The new forms of management and governmentality in science are hybridized with the assimilation of entrepreneurship as a framework for understanding the worker (Serrano & Fernández, 2018). According to this, individual capacity for adaptation, initiative and strategic investment will determine the result and value of the work. The worker is required to have a strong identification and dedication in their activity, while cooperation and sociability tend to be guided by instrumental and productivist criteria (Lynch, 2015). This leads to an individualistic tendency coexisting with a collaborative vocation, which produces a whole series of contradictions and tensions. In the same way, leadership has become more complex, fulfilling more and more functions in an increasingly accelerated and intensified scientific life. Moreover, leadership is trying to balance greater participation and horizontal relationships with a centralized direction and a common strategic vision in teams.

Nowadays, when transformations in the organization of work have been consolidated in the field of scientific-academic research, we assert that the culture of collaboration which highlights the value of interdependence both outside and within teams predominates. In the case of the youngest PIs and those who are on the highpoint of their career, this is identified with a call to more horizontal structures and affective proximity in relationships; position that is questioned by PIs with more experience and socialized in a traditional academic context, where coordinators have more authority. Following Verbree (2011), both age and generation are variables that determine leadership style and, we add, the way of understanding the role of leaders and collaboration.

This collective dimension of collaboration does not necessarily turn the group into a unified entity from the point of view of fondness and identity, but is experienced in a more complex, dynamic, and contradictory way. Thus, the group is experienced more as the background of research action than as a collective and homogeneous subject; a framework where individual lines of work are developed which, although with common objectives, only converge occasionally. As we have observed the work culture and the socio-organizational factors of research teams, we understand the distance between the collectivist ideal of collaboration and the real experience, which we know through how the workers characterize the tensions that this distance generates and how they are solved.

For Garfinkel (1967) the efforts to breach trust in cooperative stances that underlie mundane cognition and action were met with intense anger – one of the negative emotions that we have observed during our meetings and that has accompanied other negative emotions like stress. Goodwin (2007) found that moral stance becomes visible when an actor refuses to assume a cooperative stance toward the actions initiated by others and can thus generate specific forms of affective stance. Following Goodwin (2007), we can assert that visible structure of such participation frameworks enables separate individuals to build joint action together in ways that take account of both relevant structure in the environment that is the focus of their work and what each other is doing.

As in other professional fields, the emotional discourses aimed at highlighting the horizontal and collective relationships of research groups express more the attachment to a growing collaborative culture than real work organization. Emphasizing the pragmatic, dynamic and unstable character of discursive positions, and their articulation with socio-material elements, allows us to appreciate the gaps between everyday reality and discourses that tend to be hegemonic. In fact, the effort to use a more democratizing language, aimed at repairing the intrinsic contradictions of authority roles. However, it also shows that some rhetoric could mask power relations and produce communicative ambiguity (Alonso & Fernández-Rodríguez, 2013).

5.2 Emotional leadership in science

We explore scientific collaboration and the role played by leadership within research groups, especially in the management of emotions that can be observed in other professional settings. We start from the assumption that the strategies that can enhance effective, creative, and sustainable collaboration involve the management of relationships and affective tensions that can occur within the sphere of activity between individuals and the group.

Our perspective proposes to take a step further in the study of leadership and management. We relate it to management studies elements, both structural and organizational, without abandoning the framework of critical psychology and, particularly, the study of emotions. Focusing on the socio-interactive patterns within research groups, we seek to understand the changing and even contradictory circulation of influence in daily interactions, conditioned by the agency of the subjects, which in turn is shaped by the forms of leadership.

We have identified the potential to create work climates where team members can dynamically take initiative on some tasks or confer a shared sense of organization. In contrast to the determinism of formal positions, the importance of informality will be highlighted when defining interactions and positions. Likewise, we observe how leadership is related to strategy within the organization and to emotions, affective ties within the group and its daily rituals.

In the last three decades, psychological studies on organizational models and professional life have incorporated an in-depth look at affects and emotions (Ashforth & Humphrey, 1995; Ashkanasy et al., 2000; Fineman, 2003). As the work by Arlie Hochschild (1983) exposed, emotions that happen in work contexts is not an aspect that should be repressed, but rather tends to be managed vertically. Hence, emotional work can be understood many times as 'functional' to the objectives of organizations. We assume that people work with and on own emotions to meet norms or achieve goals in different contexts. We also do this in decision-making processes and leadership relationships.

Emotions too are present in the deployment of scientific collaborations. However, mainstream discourses have always stated that emotionality is something that must be separated and be watched with caution if a valid, objective and scientific result is sought. As Mahoney (1979: 364) explains, 'Scientists derive much of their motivation and professional satisfaction from their emotional involvement in their work. In a technical sense, of course, the scientist cannot be devoid of emotions'. Our interest focuses on explaining how the coordination practices of PIs of research groups deal with affective elements beyond epistemological considerations on the 'situated' and 'embodied' character of the practices of knowledge production. As interdependence and cooperation among researchers is valued more and occupies a greater role in the work of high-performance groups, it becomes pertinent to inquire into its emotional embodiment, particularly if we consider that few studies have examined this issue.

Previous work on the subject indicates that emotion management in science encompasses a wide variety of skills and areas of interaction. One of the crucial elements for productivity is the motivation of researchers (Pelz & Andrews, 1976). Both external, such as rewards, recognition and success in goals, and internal aspects, such as autonomy, challenge and stimulation of work, are conditioned by the work environment and the work of the PI (Amabile, 1993; Verbree, 2011). Likewise, PIs must anticipate and mediate in the resolution of conflicts between researchers. In fact, balancing emotional tensions that arise in these autonomous, vertical and interdependent relationships will be one of the fundamental challenges in team coordination and decision-making (Hackett, 2005; Gengler, 2020).

Among the strategies that scientific team leaders employ, we pay special attention to those that focus on conditioning the affective bonds between their participants. Research has concluded that one of the key functions of leaders is the generation of an environment that motivate dialogue and sociability as a source of creativity and innovation (Raelin, 2013). The reduction of feelings of rivalry and comparison, as well as the constitution of spheres where individuals can maintain concentration and autonomy, is also very important (Amabile, 1993; Hansson & Monsted, 2008). On the other hand, inter-trust has been investigated as a decisive factor in collaboration. This depends on emotional closeness and informal relationships, as well as on mutual knowledge and shared experience within a formal organization (McAllister, 1995).

The discourses and interviews that we have analyzed of IPs that manage research groups allows us to focus on concrete practices that take place in their local contexts of work. Daily life of offices and laboratories is full of small gestures, deference, and comments. We find signs of how most of the individuals and collective logics of scientific collaboration operates. Within these practices, the central character of the PI's coordination work can be seen in the ways participants interact. In a research group, the coordinator's orientations can modulate tendencies towards a more individual or collective logic. An important dimension of these strategies is 'emotional labour' (Hochschild, 1983).

The different strategies that PIs highlight show that in the search for a balance between the individual and the group, it is important to combine an affective activation, that is, the mobilization of positive and spontaneous affections. This is obtained through, generally, proximity and warmth. Also by affective deactivation, through moderation and reduction of intense feelings, usually thanks to coldness or emotional distancing.

The IP must ensure the presence of affective networks that not only reinforce individual work, but also empower the group as a whole, enhancing group identity. He can reach this goal making positive reinforcements to all the members of the team as a whole. As it is repeatedly present in the interviews and in the observations, motivational functions rely largely on an 'emotional socialization' that is anchored in daily interactions such as spontaneous comments, supportive gestures or, even, micro-strategies planned by the IPs.

Emotional control also operates on group logic, as a whole, making use of formal patterns that are more or less conventional. Many times, it consists of ensuring that certain contexts adapt to behaviour rules that do not motivate excessively colloquial expressions: joking tones, lack of rigour in language, non-academic contexts .... In order to promote it, they must create an emotional basement. It consists of two intertwined movements: affective activation and deactivation through different types of strategies. IPs have the capacity to promote these dynamics by performing emotional work. On the one hand, they must foster affective bonds and an inter-subjective proximity. On the other hand, they must cool these ties through a certain formality (for example, through what we call 'rituals'). This double dynamic is exerted through two logics that IPs must balance in their groups: ego-centred and group.

The emotional work of the IP implies enlivening a warmth and spontaneity that motivates researchers and generates the desire to work together, whilst at the same time requires cooling emotional intensity, in order to prevent conflicts and the clash of strong personalities, maintaining a formal code of reference. With these ideas, we join Hackett's theory (2005) on the existence of an essential tension in science between autonomy and democratic participation.

5.3 Conclusion

Researchers, academics, scientists, and so on, need to manage their emotions in their professional activities, they need to invest themselves emotionally in a new venture that represents their aspirations and passions so that they are emotionally embodied with a project. Of course it is not only the emotions and passions that ensure a project will have success, but it is also important to be able to put the idea in an intellectual and logical order from this first emotional investment. Researchers must organize the results of their experience to present the project to the scientific community. Working together requires a substantial investment of time, emotions, and intellect, when effective teamwork is a stake, it is unsurprising that much work is concerned with how to enhance the success of collaborations (Pardee et al., 2018; Darics & Gatti, 2019). Advice for members to create a sense of connectedness and equality (Boros et al., 2010), focusing more on social interactions (Suh & Shin, 2010) or maintaining a close working relationship (White, 2014). Conflict resolution, planning, or negotiation, where the ambiguity of the information and the requirement for rapid clarification and feedback are critical for the success of the interaction (Daft & Lengel, 1984; Whittaker, 1992). We understand these emotions as a way to access the meaning patterns that users apply in their relationship.

We have presented in this chapter emotions from a relational perspective, focusing our attention on the relationship with others and the context. As in Hochschild (1979), we will observe how certain emotions in certain social contexts are created, the so called 'feeling rules'. This interactive organization of embodied participation constructed by talk and gestures is the basis of the collaborative activity. It represents a demonstration of the work of participants and environment to show the cooperation in the joint accomplishment of the activity in progress.

We agree with Latour (2017); we believe that scientific research is confronted with the greed of industrialists, but we simply say the same thing as the purest capitalists; research is a cycle of capital, statements, like situations, have no value by themselves, only the reproduction and extension of the cycle counts. For these reasons we have highlighted in the last chapter of this book a very common context among all scientists and also professionals in other fields where these ambivalent emotions are generated.

The sciences are developed by applying ordinary skills to new subjects, just as the baker produces bread or buns by applying ordinary labour to bread or bun dough. Without a doubt, professional customs end up creating bodies so selectively trained that they can end up diverging, to the point that one can distinguish a morning baker with flour-covered arms from a night-owl mathematician with chalk-stained hands. But the small differences of trade are not so great that epistemologists mount a whole number and come to separate 'explicit knowledge' from the poor 'implicit savoir-faire'. The scientific work to unfold, make explicit and soften the inscriptions seems to us implicit in itself, intricate, obscure, trained in a practice that until recently hardly anyone knew how to study.

If one wanted to summarize in one sentence the recent transformation of the philosophy of science that this report on images illustrates, it would have to be said that knowledge has become savoir-faire (Latour, 2017).

References

Alonso, L.E., & Fernández-Rodríguez, C. (2018). *Poder y sacrificio*. Los nuevos discursos de la empresa. Madrid: Siglo XXI.

Amabile, T.M. (1993). Motivation synergy: toward new conceptualizations of intrinsic and extrinsic motivation in the workplace. *Human Resource Management Review*, 3(3), 185–201.

Ashforth, B. & Humphrey, R. (1995). Emotion in the workplace: A reappraisal. *Human Relations*, 48(2), 97–125. https://doi.org/10.1177/001872679504800201

Ashkanasy, N.M., Hartel, C.E.J. & Zerbe, W. (2000). *Emotions in the Workplace: Research, Theory and Practice*. Westport, CT: Quorum.

Boltanski, L., & Chiapello, E. (2002). *El nuevo espíritu del capitalismo*. Madrid: Akal.

Boros, S., Meslec, N., Curseu, P.L., et al. (2010). Struggles for cooperation: Conflict resolution strategies in multicultural groups. *Journal of Managerial Psychology*, 25: 539–554.

Cannizzo, F. (2017).'You've got to love what you do': Academic labor in a culture of authenticity. *The Sociological Review*, 66(1), 91–106.

Daft, R., and Lengel, R. (1984). Information richness: A new approach to managerial behavior and organizational design. In B. Straw and L. Cummings (eds.), *Research in Organizational Behavior* (pp.191–223). JAI Press, Greenwich, CT.

Darics, E., & Cristina Gatti, M. (2019). Talking a team into being in online workplace collaborations: The discourse of virtual work. *Discourse Studies*, 21(3), 237–257.

Fernández Porta, E. (2022). *Los brotes negros*, Barcelona, Anagrama.

Fineman, S. (2003). *Understanding Emotion at Work*. London: SAGE.

Fisher, M. (2016). *Realismo capitalista*. Buenos Aires: Caja Negra.

Garfinkel, H. (1967). *Studies in Ethnomethodology*. Prentice Hall, New York.

Gengler, A.M. (2020). Emotions and Medical Decision-Making. *Social Psychology Quarterly*, 83(2), 174–194. https://doi.org/10.1177%2F0190272519876937

Goodwin, C. (2007). Participation, stance and affect in the organization of activities. *Discourse & Society*, 18(1), 53–73.

Hackett, E.J. (2005). Essential tensions: Identity, control, and risk in research. *Social Studies of Science*, 35(5), 787–826. https://doi.org/10.1177/0306312705056045

Hansson, F.; Monsted, M. (2008). Research leadership as entrepreneurial organizing for research. *Higher Education*, 55, 651–670. https://doi.org/10.1007/s10734-007-9081-5

Hochschild, A. (1979). Emotion work, feeling rules and social structure. *The American Journal of Sociology*, 85 (November), 551–575.

Hochschild, A.R. (1983) *The Managed Heart: Commercialization of Human Feeling*. Berkeley, CA: University of California Press.

Latour, B. (2017). *Lecciones de sociología de las ciencias*. Madrid: Arpa Editores.

Lupton, D., Mewburn, I., & Thomson, P. (2017). *The Digital Academic: Critical Perspectives on Digital Technologies in Higher Education*. New York: Routledge.

Lynch, K. (2015). Control by Numbers: A New Managerialism and Ranking in Higher Education. *Critical Studies in Education*, 56(2), 190–207. https://doi.org/10.1080/17508487.2014.949811

Mahoney, J. (1979). Psychology of the Scientist: An Evaluative Review, *Social Studies of Science*, 9, 349–376. https://doi.org/10.1177/030631277900900304

McAllister, D.J. (1995). Affect- and cognition-based trust as foundations for interpersonal cooperation in organizations. *Academy of Management Journal*, 38(1), 24–59. https://doi.org/10.2307/256727

Pardee, J.W., Fothergill, A., Weber, L., & Peek, L. (2018). The collective method: collaborative social science research and scholarly accountability. *Qualitative Research*, 18(6), 671–688.

Pelz, D.C. & Andrews, F.M. (1976). *Scientists in Organizations: Productive Climates for Research and Development*. Michigan: Institute for Social Research.

Raelin, J.A. (2013). The manager as facilitator of dialogue. *Organization*, 20(6), 818–839. https://doi.org/10.1177/1350508412455085

Ranieri, V., Barratt, H., Fulop, N., & Rees, G. (2016). Factors that influence career progression among postdoctoral clinical academics: a scoping review of the literature. *BMJ Open*, 6(10), 1–7.

Rodríguez López, R., Borges Gómez, E. (2018). El perfil del emprendedor. Construcción cultural de la subjetividad laboral postfordista. *Cuadernos De Relaciones Laborales*, 36(2), 265–284.

Ross, A. (2000). The mental labour problem. *Social Text*, 18(2), 7–34.

Santos Ortega, A., Serrano-Pascual, A., Borges, E. (2021). El dispositivo emprendedor: Interpelación ética y producción de nuevos sujetos del trabajo. *Revista Española de Sociología*, 30(3), a62. https://doi.org/10.22325/fes/res.2021.62

Sennett, R. (2012). *Together. The Rituals, Pleasures and Politics of Cooperation*. New Haven: Yale University Press.

Serrano-Pascual, A., & Fernández-Rodríguez, C.J. (2018). De la metáfora del mercado a la sinécdoque del emprendedor: la reconfiguración política del modelo referencial de trabajador. *Cuadernos de Relaciones Laborales*, 36(2), 207–224.

Suh, A. & Shin, K-S. (2010). Exploring the effects of online social ties on knowledge sharing: A comparative analysis of collocated vs. dispersed teams. *Journal of Information Science*, 36, 443–463.

Verbree, M. (2011). *Dynamics of Academic Leadership in Research Groups*. Den Haag: Rathenau Instituut.

White, M. (2014). The management of virtual teams and virtual meetings. *Business Information Review*, 31(2), 111–117.

Whittaker, S. (1992). Towards a theory of mediated communication. Unpublished manuscript.

Zafra, R. (2017). *El entusiasmo. Precariedad y trabajo creativo en la era digital*. Barcelona: Anagrama.

CONCLUSION

Questions about the nature and purpose of emotions have puzzled scholars for millennia (van Kleef & Cote, 2022). They permeated the thinking of ancient philosophers, divided influential thinkers, and catalyzed the inception of the scientific discipline of psychology. Emotions pervade our personal and professional lives, shape our relationships and social interactions, and influence our work performance and general life (van Kleef & Cote, 2022).

In these five chapters, we have presented five different turns in the recent scientific contributions in the field of critical psychology of emotions. We have also showed the impact they have had in different contexts. It is evident that the study of emotions is even more complex if we consider the digital environment that this line of research has recently incorporated. Probably in this new context, the density of emotions is represented by the complexity of the language used in online communication, in which users do not use body language or facial strategies to express themselves. We must be prepared as researchers in the field of emotions to face these novelties due to the increased use of digital tools, which draws a new graphic representation of emotions that, with great certainty, will be the focus of new studies in the coming decades.

In the first chapter, we have seen how an emotional performance, such as love, changes through historical discourse. Thanks to the concept of performance, emotions are not something fixed, defined, and static. They are constantly evolving, continuously complying with an iteration process, and they do it through language, natural and subjective. This constant iteration makes emotions appear and disappear from the discursive arena, leaving some forgotten and discovering new others. We consider emotions as a constant evolution in daily discourse.

In the second chapter, we have seen how the emotional affordance is key to understanding how materiality affects the practice of the users, adapting digital settings to suit certain tasks for users who work frequently with technologies as a

DOI: 10.4324/9781003247999-7

combined part of their work. We suggested the term emotional affordance to better incorporate the emotional aspects of technological artefacts, keeping an eye on the qualities of technological environments to move towards more nuanced theories at the intersection of social processes and technological materiality.

In the third chapter, we have been able to observe how in recent years online communication has introduced a different grammar of emotions, where researchers rediscover the important role that emotions play in communication between users who share the same 'emotional dictionary'. We must be prepared as researchers in the field of emotions, that due to the great increase in these digital tools, a new graphic representation of emotions, with great security, will be the focus of new studies in the coming decades. We have observed how the most elementary thing in these new contexts is emotional expression, and therefore one of the great challenges for the future will be to develop a methodology to monitor the constant possibility of recording the way in which these emotions arise in a precise moment.

In the fourth chapter, we have observed that collective emotions and emotional contagion can occur at many different levels, including social comparison processes in which people evaluate their emotions in comparison with or influenced by others and respond with what seems appropriate in the setting, calling this 'contagion' in the same way that epidemiologists do it.

In the last chapter, we have presented emotions from a relational perspective, focusing our attention on the relationship with others and the context. This interactive organization of embodied participation constructed by talk and gestures is the basis of the collaborative activity. It represents a demonstration of the work of participants and environment to show the cooperation in the joint accomplishment of the activity in progress.

Through this book, we have noticed how the performance and the affordance of emotions, that is, the expression, intensity, and manifestations of these, are transformed over time and across cultures through our discursive productions. We have appreciated how emotional contagion has focused mainly on social participation and in pandemic times. Both have obviously had a great impact on all spheres of our lives, not only emotionally, but always sharing what characterizes the human being and being in society which is feeling emotions and sharing them with others. Extending the invitation of Arlie Hochschild (2019), we share that feeling that those emotions are 'out there', from the global mobilizations against climate change to the transnational journeys of refugees, war conflicts, and catastrophes. These are different stories and narratives that are worth studying to understand what problems and questions the study of emotions should find answers to.

References

Hochschild, A. (2019). Emotions and society. *Emotions and Society*, 1(1), 9–13. https://doi.org/10.1332/263168919X15580836411805

van Kleef, G. A., & Côté, S. (2022). The social effects of emotions. *Annual Review of Psychology*, 73(1), 629–658. https://doi.org/10.1146/annurev-psych-020821-010855

INDEX

Academia.edu 69
active ageing, idea of 36
Actor-Network Theory (ANT) 22, 57
affordance: concept of 2, 19, 20–1; of digital technology 21; discursive 21; emotional 21–5; new context for sharing emotions 33–4; response-dependent component 21; rhetorical 21; between social construction and technological determinism 20; in social interactions 19; socio-material turn 20; technological 20, 22
affordance ability, awareness of 23
Agamben, Giorgio 14
anxiety 11, 23
anxiety-depressive symptoms 40
Austin, John 12; *How to Do Things with Words* (1955) 12; on types of acts that can be done with words 12
awareness of intimacy 53

banalization of sex 35
Baricco, Alessandro 35
Bauman, Zygmunt 35, 59
behaviour privacy 38
being dangerous, notion of 21
biological reductionism, rise of 5
blogs 33
bodily attunement, modes of 26
body-hacking 36
body language 77
body–speech relationship 13

breach of trust 71
business communication techniques 69
business management practices 70
business reasoning, representations of 69
Butler, Judith 12, 16

capitalist cultural grammar 36
career and collaboration, in research 67–71
career satisfaction 67
causal accounts, in emotional narratives 9–10
clinical psychology 40
cognitive component, of emotion 42
cognitive-semantics 11
collaborative practices, complexity and heterogeneity of 68
collective emotions 52, 61; defined 53; features of 53; group-based 53; and movements 52–6; social dynamics of 61
collective rituals 52, 53
communication between users, role of emotions in 42
complexity of emotions 42
components of emotions 42
construction of the emotion 7–8
corporal responses, in emotions 19
counterimitation, process of 57
COVID-19 pandemic 56, 58–60
critical psychology 32; developments in 3; of emotions 1
cultural industry 36
cybernetic spaces 33

data processing, impact of anxiety on 23
decision-making 72
digital academics 69
digital community, fear of relating to 37
digital dating 35
digital interactions 43
digital mediations, in information management and communication 69
digital practices 37
digital social networks 31
digital spaces 25; fear of sharing 37; of social interaction 42
digital technologies 19, 32; affordances of 21; emotions associated with 42; interaction with humans 23; research on emotional affordance using 22
digital tools, use of 77
digital transformation 19, 37, 42
digital turn 43, 44
disciplines, in the study of emotions 5
discursive psychology of emotion 11, 44
discursive turn, from the philosophy of emotion 4–6
dodo, story of 21
Dropbox 22

Edwards, Derek 21
ego-centred emotions 73
emo-grammar 42, 44
emojis, use of 43
EMOTEX model 41
emoticons: etymology of 43; used to convey emotional content in digital settings 43
emotions: associated with digital technologies 42; bodily experience 14; definitions of 5–6; hybrid theory 41–4; iconography of 42; impact on natural and spontaneous language of everyday life 15; recognition of 41; as socially constructed phenomena 13; sociocultural contexts of 14
emotional affordance 20, 24, 77–8; of digital environments 27; notion of 21–2; patterns of good and bad connections 22; research using digital technology 22; social approaches to 22–3; social demonstrations of 21; in social networks 23–5; social responses to conflicting events 21; socio-material turn 21; technology and 22–3
emotional attachment 27; based on trust 53
emotional capitalism 37
emotional connection, in the socio-material network 22–3

emotional contagion 3, 61, 78; concept of 58–9; as contagion based on the textual rather than on the body 59; expressed in digital contexts 59; influence on people behaviour during COVID-19 pandemic 56; at macro level 58; at micro level 58; transfer of emotions through 57; use in political evaluations of individuals 58
emotional development 10
emotional dictionary 44, 78
emotional discourse 15
emotional engineering 68
emotional experience, elements of 11
emotional expression 7
emotional intelligence, rise of 68
emotional labour 73
emotional leadership, in science 71–4
emotional narratives 9
emotional performance 7, 77
emotional processes, in socio-material network 20
emotional recovery 25
emotional security 33
emotional self-control, demand for 37
emotional situations 23
emotional socialization 73
emotional speech, effects of 11
emotional synchrony 53
emotional vocabulary, use of 41
emotion grammar 9
emotions–language relationship: discursive psychology of 11; discursive turn in 4–6; philosophical and psychological character of 6–7; social and discursive practices 4; social character of mind and 8
emotions–time relationship 13–15
emotion work concept of 10
employment activation 36

Facebook 23, 24, 25, 33, 38, 42
facial expressions, mimicry of 56
fear and trust, notion of 59–61
fear of death, emotion of 11
fear of missing out 25
feeling rules 74
feelings of rivalry and comparison 73
first-person plural consciousness 53
Fisher, Mark 68
folk psychology 8
Fox, Aaron 55
free market, of sexual encounters 35
Fridays For Future movement 61

Index

gamification of our emotions 34–7, 70
generation of emotions 42
generative imitation, meaning of 57
Goffman, Erving 60
Goldie, Peter 5, 9, 11
good and bad connections, idea of 22
Google Docs 22
government, temporalization of 26
grammar of emotions 44
group-based emotions 53, 61, 73

happiness: idea of 26; industry of 36; instrumentalization of 26; notion of 25; psychology of 25, 32–3
happiness turn, notion of 31
Harré, Rom 5, 9, 11, 56
healthy emotional balance 37
hedonic adaptation, principle of 31
heterosexual romantic relationship 36
Hochschild, Arlie 5, 72, 78
How to Do Things with Words (1955) 12
Hufendiek, R. 20, 21
humanities 6
human relationships, functioning of 42
human–technology interactions 23; psychological and social characteristics of 27
hybrid theory, of emotions 41–4

iconography of emotions 42
illocutionary act 12
imitative imitation 57
I-mode emotions 54–5
implicit savoir-faire 75
information exchange 58
information processing 58
Instagram 24, 38, 39
interpersonal behaviours 53
interpersonal cognitive processes 52
intimate relationships, commodification of 35

joint attention, importance of 56
joint emotions 61

Kernowicz, Pierre 66
knowledge production, practices of 72

language, complexity of 42
Latour, Bruno 22, 66, 74; idea of good and bad connections 22
linguistic articulations, of our feelings and impressions 7
LinkedIn 69

liquid fear, concept of 59
locutionary act 12
loved person, loss of 10
love stories 15
Lyons, William 6

meta-emotions 10; anxiety 11
microblogging 33
Middle Ages 14
moral feelings 5
motivated cognitive processing, theory of 58
motivated political reasoning, theory of 58
music, physical representation of emotions with 55

Naïve Bayes algorithm 41
narratives of emotions 8–11
natural language processing, linguistic method of 41
negative emotions, public disclosure of 34
neoliberal economy 26
Netflix 35–6
networked individualism, concept of 36
networked public 39
network of intimacy 36
Newsweek 24
non-reciprocal tracking 38
non-verbal behaviour 43
non-verbal gestures 15

Oatley, Keith 7
Occupy movement (2011) 53, 61
offline interactions 43
online and offline space, division between 42
online communication 42
online dating 35–6, 70
online identities 37
online interactions, ethnomethodology and conversational analysis 43
online relationships 36

painful emotions, management of 10
Parchoma, G. 20
Parker, Ian 32
performance: concept of 12, 19; 'happy' utterances 12
performance, concept of 77
performative perspective of emotions 11–13
performativity in language: concept of 12; construction of 13; politics of 13
perlocutionary act, idea of 12, 44

phenomenon of emotion 13
physiological component, of emotion 42
physiological reactions 10
plastic sexuality 36
political rationalities, transformation of 36
Porta, Fernández 69
'positive' emotions, in influencing social relations 25
positive psychology 25, 26
pride–shame relationship 10
principal investigators (PIs) 69, 70, 72
private communication channels, use of 38
problem-solving processes 68
productive networks 69
professional identity 68
professional interactions 66
professional networks 69
psychological individuality, notion of 32
psychological regulation, to a rationality 26
psychological research programme 14
psychology of emotions 3, 7, 77; cognitive-semantic model 11; role in building tools and digital environments 23; social constructionist model 11; study of 11–12
punctuation marks, used to convey facial expressions 43

qualities for communication and sharing 22
quality of life 33
quantified self, notion of 36

recognition of emotions 41
regulation of emotions 5–6
Researchgate 69
research groups, management of 69
rhetorical affordance, concept of 21
romantic encounters, principle of 36

sadness, concept of 9
scientific collaborations 66
self-assessment 36
self-esteem 33
self-exploitation, mechanisms of 70
self-expressive behaviours 34
self-governance 35
self-regulation, emotional 37
Sennett, Richard 69
shared message, magnitude of 38
sharing emotions: process of 19; in society 52
social and discursive practices 6
social beliefs and values, endorsement of 53
social component, of emotion 42

social construction: of daily relationships 31; of emotion 8
social constructionism 4
social, definition of 5
social demonstrations 21
social emotion, from relationships and attachments 10
social gatherings 60
social interaction, digital space of 42
social iterative speech, theory of 13
socialization, processes of 43
social media 2, 33
social networks 34, 38, 42, 58, 69; emotional affordance in 23–5; emotional component of 41; emotions in 37–41; functionality of 39; popularity of 41; use of 33
social ontology 54
social privacy 24
social psychology 23; definition of 31; of emotions 5, 44
social relationships, construction of 43
social reproduction of customs, mode of 57
social resilience 60
social sciences 6
social turn of emotions 52
sociocultural structure, in the generation of emotions 5
socio-digital discrimination 43
socio-material network 22; emotional connection in 22–3
socio-material turn of emotions 19, 21
socio-professional relationships 69
speaking about oneself, process of 2, 4
Spinoza's concept of emotions 6
structured episodes 10
study of emotions, complexity of 4

talent development 70
Tarde, Gabriel 56–7
technological affordance: emotional strength of 22–3; notion of 20, 22; social approaches to 22
technological artefacts, use of 27
technological environments, qualities of 27
technological innovations, political and social consequences of 20
technological materiality 27
technological objects, characteristics of 23
testing emotions, process of 2, 42

therapeutic intervention, notion of 36
Tinder's digital space 25
T-PIECE model 41
Tuomela, R. 54
Twitter 24, 38–42, 44

University of Chicago 15

value-free physical object 20
video presentations 42
video-sharing 33

virtual social identities, construction of 37
Vygotsky, Lev 13–14

Weber, Max 59
well-being, feeling of 40
We-mode emotions 54
Wetherell, Margaret 56
WhatsApp 38
Wittgenstein, L. 7

Zuckerberg, Mark 24

Printed in the United States
by Baker & Taylor Publisher Services